TRUMP

Worst. President. Ever.

Author of 555 Ways to Get Revenge
BEAU STEVENS

Layout by Beau Stevens

Photo editing by Beau Stevens

All photos common license unless otherwise noted.

Printed in the United States of America

Copyright ©2021 by Smoke Alarm Media

ISBN: 978-1-927458-35-8

All facts for this book were verified with publicly-available, reputable sources.

It might be difficult to believe, but this is a true story.

Sadly.

FOREWARD

DONALD TRUMP, A RETROSPECTIVE: A LOOK BACK AT THE 1,462 WORST DAYS IN PRESIDENTIAL HISTORY

BY BESS LEVIN, *Vanity Fair*

By Wednesday afternoon, January 20, 2021, Donald Trump will be 992 miles from the White House, ensconced at his Palm Beach resort where his neighbors hate his guts. Joe Biden will have taken the oath of office and Americans will no longer have to worry about the possibility that the president of the United States is a crook, or trying to get them killed, or a friend of neo-Nazis, or an ugly racist, or paying off porn stars, or putting his idiot children in charge of national emergencies, or hiring a dog breeder to head up a coronavirus task force. Oh, did you forget about that last one? Or about the time the Trump administration threatened to economically cripple Ecuador for promoting breastfeeding? Or when Trump went on an unhinged rant in front of 35,000 children? Or when he hired an acting Attorney General who worked for a company that marketed "masculine toilets"? It's understandable that, with all the impeachment and extortion and coronavirus and sedition, you might have forgotten. But as a reminder, and so grade school students hundreds of years from now are told, here's a look back at the the worst president in American history, through the headlines.

In the end Trump was not forcibly removed from the White House despite posing a clear and present danger to society, but he was the first president in history to be impeached twice. He may also become the first president to both actually be convicted by the Senate and perhaps a court of law. Also the first one to kill 400,000 people and, separately, incite an act of sedition! Can't forget that.

....

June 16, 2015

Trump formally announced his candidacy with a campaign rally and speech at Trump Tower in New York City. The campaign slogan was announced as "Make America Great Again." *The Hollywood Reporter* reported that a casting company had offered $50 to actors to attend the Trump event, "to wear t-shirts and carry signs and help cheer him in support of his announcement."

July 6, 2015

Trump issues a statement, claiming that the Mexican government is "forcing their most unwanted people into the United States"—"in many cases, criminals, drug dealers, rapists, etc."

July 18, 2015

At an event Trump described John McCain as a "loser" and added, "He's not a war hero. He was a war hero because he was captured. I like people who weren't captured." His comments were heavily criticized; some of his primary rivals said he should withdraw from the race because of them. McCain said Trump should apologize, not to him personally, but to former American prisoners of war and "the families of those who have sacrificed in conflict". Trump declined to issue any apology.

July 22, 2015

The Federal Election Commission released details of Trump's wealth and financial holdings, which he had submitted to them when he became a Republican presidential candidate. The report showed assets above $1.4 billion and outstanding debts of at least $265 million. Shortly afterwards, Trump's campaign released a statement stating that his net worth is over $10 billion,

July 23, 2015

Trump visited the Mexican border and planned to meet with border guards. The meeting did not take place due to the intervention of the labor union of the U.S. Customs and Border Protection guards, who refused to meet with him.

August 8, 2015

In a televised debate, Fox News anchor Megyn Kelly asked about how Trump would respond to the Clinton campaign saying that he was waging a "war on women". Trump replied, "I think the big problem this country has is being politically correct."
In a later interview with Don Lemon on CNN Tonight, Trump said that Kelly is a "lightweight" and had "blood coming out of her eyes, blood coming out of her ... wherever." Trump tweeted that his remark referred to Kelly's nose but was interpreted by critics as a reference to menstruation.

TRUMP: *Worst. President. Ever.*

October 16, 2015

Trump promoted the discredited belief that vaccines can cause autism.

....

November 15, 2015

In remarks made following the November 2015 Paris attacks, Trump stated that he would support a database for tracking Muslims in the United States and expanded surveillance of mosques. Trump's support for an American Muslim database drew sharp rebukes from his Republican presidential rivals and disbelief from legal experts

....

November 12, 2015

Within six months of Trump's announcement of his presidential campaign, FactCheck.org declared Trump the "King of Whoppers" stating, "In the 12 years of FactCheck.org's existence, we've never seen his match. He stands out not only for the sheer number of his factually false claims, but also for his brazen refusals to admit error when proven wrong."

..

November 22, 2015

Trump said of a protester in Birmingham, Alabama, "Maybe he should have been roughed up, because it was absolutely disgusting what he was doing."

....

December 7, 2015

In response to the 2015 San Bernardino attack, Trump further called for a temporary ban on any Muslims entering the country. He issued a written statement saying, "Donald J. Trump is calling for a total and complete shutdown of Muslims entering the United States until our country's representatives can figure out what is going on," which he repeated at subsequent political rallies.

....

December 18, 2015

Trump praised Russia's Vladimir Putin, calling him a strong leader, "unlike what we have in this country...a man so highly respected within his own country and beyond," and wondered if "he will become my new best friend."

....

December 21, 2015

Politifact named "the many campaign misstatements of Donald Trump" as its "2015 Lie of the Year", noting at the time that 76 percent of Trump statements rated by the factchecking website were rated "Mostly False, False or Pants on Fire", more than any other politician.

....

January 10, 2016

Trump commented on North Korean leader Kim Jong-un, first saying he's a "maniac", but then stating "you gotta give him credit" for the "incredible" way he eliminated his opponents to take charge of the country.

....

TRUMP: *Worst. President. Ever.*

2016

February 1, 2016

In Cedar Rapids, Iowa, Trump told the crowd there might be tomato-throwing protesters, and urged his audience to "knock the crap out of 'em" if anyone should try. "I promise you, I will pay the legal fees", he added.

February 23, 2016

At a rally in Las Vegas, Trump reacted to a protester by saying "I love the old days—you know what they used to do to guys like that when they were in a place like this? They'd be carried out on a stretcher, folks", adding "I'd like to punch him in the face."

February 24, 2016

David Duke, a former Ku Klux Klan Grand Dragon, expressed vocal support for Trump's campaign on his radio show.

March 3, 2016

An open letter from 120 conservative foreign-policy and national-security leaders is released, condemning Trump as "fundamentally dishonest" and unfit to be president.

March 3, 2016

Republican senator Mitt Romney said that Trump's economic plans would cause profound recession, criticized his foreign policy proposals as reckless and dangerous, and called him a "con man", a "fake", and a "phony", joking that Trump's promises are "as worthless as a degree from Trump University".

March 9, 2016

A Trump supporter was charged with assault after he sucker-punched a protester who was being led out of the event. When Trump was asked if he would pay the man's legal fees, Trump said he was "looking into it". The local sheriff's office considered filing charges against Trump for "inciting a riot" at that event.

March 18, 2016

Trump resumed his feud with Fox News and Megyn Kelly in a number of Twitter messages disparaging Kelly and calling for a boycott of her show. Fox News responded with a statement saying that Trump's behavior was an "extreme, sick obsession" beneath the dignity of a presidential nominee.

April 23, 2016

In the early days of the primary, Senator Ted Cruz showered praise on Trump. But as the primary season went on, Cruz went on the attack, calling Trump a "bully" and a "pathological liar", and Trump took to referring to Cruz as "Lyin' Ted". Trump repeatedly claimed Cruz was not eligible to be

TRUMP: *Worst. President. Ever.*

president because he was born in Canada.

....

May 3, 2016

Trump became the presumptive nominee of the Republican Party after his victory in Indiana and the withdrawal of the last competitors, Ted Cruz and John Kasich, from the race.

....

May 23, 2016

Republican Senator Lindsey Graham, a primary rival, was "one of Trump's fiercest critics". He called Trump a "race-baiting, xenophobic, religious bigot" and asserted that Trump doesn't have the temperament or judgment to be president. After Trump attacked a federal judge for his Mexican heritage, Graham urged people who had endorsed Trump to rescind their endorsements, saying "This is the most un-American thing from a politician since Joe McCarthy." Graham stated that he would vote for neither Trump nor Clinton.

....

May 3, 2016

Mitt Romney expressed concern that some of the things Trump says could legitimize racism, and that Trump as president could cause "trickle-down racism, trickle-down bigotry, trickle-down misogyny, all these things (that) are extraordinarily dangerous to the heart and character of America"

....

July 5, 2016

At a campaign rally, Trump again raised controversy by praising Saddam Hussein for being good at killing terrorists, saying Hussein was "a really bad guy" but "you know what he did well? He killed terrorists. He did that so good. They didn't read them the rights. They didn't talk. They were terrorists. It was over." *The New York Times* said that Trump's descriptions "are not grounded in fact", noting that Saddam Hussein's Iraq itself had been listed as a state sponsor of terrorism.

....

August 8, 2016

In a televised debate, Fox News anchor Megyn Kelly asked about how Trump would respond to the Clinton campaign saying that he was waging a "war on women". Trump replied, "I think the big problem this country has is being politically correct."
In a later interview with Don Lemon on CNN Tonight, Trump said that Kelly is a "lightweight" and had "blood coming out of her eyes, blood coming out of her ... wherever." Trump tweeted that his remark referred to Kelly's nose but was interpreted by critics as a reference to menstruation.

....

TRUMP: *Worst. President. Ever.*

October 7, 2016

During the 2016 United States presidential election, *The Washington Post* published a video about then-presidential candidate Donald Trump and television host Billy Bush having "an extremely lewd conversation about women". Trump described his attempt to seduce a married woman and indicated he might start kissing a woman that he and Bush were about to meet. He added, "I don't even wait. And when you're a star, they let you do it. You can do anything. ... Grab 'em by the pussy. You can do anything." Commentators and lawyers have described such an action as sexual assault. In a YouGov survey, only 19 percent of Republicans thought sexual assault would disqualify Trump from the presidency.

October 7, 2016

USA Today, which never had endorsed

any candidate in its 34-year history, broke the tradition and took sides in the race with an editorial that had declared Trump to be "erratic", described his business career as "checkered", and called him a "serial liar" and "unfit for the presidency".

October 12, 2016

Donald Trump's personal lawyer Michael Cohen paid adult film star Stormy Daniels $130,000 in hush money to deny that she had an affair with Trump. Trump would later reimburs Cohen.

October 18, 2016

Trump repeatedly urged his supporters to volunteer as poll watchers on Election Day, saying they were needed to guard against "voter fraud" and a "rigged" outcome. The rhetoric was seen as a call to intimidate minority voters or challenge their credentials to prevent them from voting.

November 1, 2016

The *Wall Street Journal* published an open letter signed by 370 economists, including eight Nobel laureates, who stated that Trump would be a "dangerous, destructive" choice for president and which encouraged voters to vote for some other candidate. The letter stated that Trump "misinforms the electorate, degrades trust in public institutions with conspiracy theories, and promotes willful delusion over engagement with reality"; that "If elected, he poses a unique danger (...) to

TRUMP: *Worst. President. Ever.*

the prosperity of the country"; and that he "promotes magical thinking and conspiracy theories over sober assessments of feasible economic policy options".

November 8, 2016

As the results came in on election night, November 8, 2016, Trump won in multiple states that had been predicted to go to Hillary Clinton. In the early morning hours of November 9, media sources declared Trump the winner of the presidency. In the nationwide popular vote, Clinton received over 2.8 million (2.1%) more votes than Trump. This is the biggest-ever loss in the popular vote for a candidate who won the election.

November 9, 2016

Students walked out of classes in schools across the country—like Washington, D.C., Denver, Omaha, Los Angeles, Phoenix, Seattle and other cities—beginning November 9, the day after the election, and continued into the following week.

January 20, 2017

45th President Donald Trump and 48th Vice President Mike Pence take the Oath of Office.

January 21, 2017

Four million people around the world attend the Women's March protesting the new administration. It was the largest single-day protest in U.S. history.

January 21, 2017

White House Press Secretary Sean Spicer accuses the media of inaccurately representing the presidential inauguration attendance. It is later proven that Trump's inauguration was one-third the size of President Obama's in 2009.

January 22, 2017

Despite repeated assurances that he will if elected, the White House announces that they will not release President Trump's tax returns.

January 23, 2017

President Trump signs three memoranda. The first withdraws the United States from the Trans-Pacific Partnership.

January 23, 2017

President Trump claims that 3–5 million illegal votes cost him the popular vote in a private meeting with congressional leaders. Virtually no evidence of fraud is found.

January 25, 2017

President Trump issues an Executive Order to begin construction of a wall on the Mexico–United States border. Mexican President Enrique Peña Nieto rejects the idea that Mexico would pay for any border wall between the United States and his country, despite Trump's promises that he would.

January 25, 2017

President Trump bans United States Environmental Protection Agency employees from contact with journalists or engagement on social media.

January 27, 2017

President Trump signs Executive Order 13769, suspending the Refugee Admissions Program for 120 days and denying entry to citizens of Iraq, Iran, Libya, Somalia, Sudan, Syria, and Yemen for 90 days

January 29, 2017

The Yakla raid, the first commando raid authorized by President Trump, leads to the death of Chief petty officer William Owens, and is considered a failure. The Obama administration had previously refused to approve the raid.

January 30, 2017

President Trump fires acting Attorney General Sally Yates after she ordered employees of the Department of Justice not to enforce the President's ban due to doubts over its legality.

February 3, 2017

Trump-appointed Federal Communications Commission chairman revokes an agreement with internet service providers for cheaper internet for poor communities.

February 7, 2017

The President falsely claims that the murder-rate in America is at a 47-year-high.

February 8, 2017

The President publicly chastises Nordstrom for not carrying his daughter Ivanka Trump's brand.

February 14, 2017

FBI Director James Comey and other officials give President Trump a briefing on counter-terrorism in the Oval Office.Trump speaks to Comey one-on-one about the FBI investigation of Mike Flynn, saying "I hope you can let this go".

February 16, 2017

The United States Department of Agriculture is instructed to replace the term 'climate change' with 'weather extremes' and 'reduce greenhouse gases' with 'build soil organic matter, increase nutrient use efficiency' and noting to staff that climate change should no longer be a priority.

....

February 17, 2017

President Trump describes on Twitter a wide range of mainstream news organizations as "the enemy of the American people".

....

February 19, 2017

The Trump administration asks the Council of Economic Advisers to predict 3.5% annual GDP growth, while the Federal Reserve had predicted 1.8%, just over half that.

....

February 22, 2017

The Trump administration rescinds a bathroom policy for transgender students that had been instated by the Obama administration.

....

February 23, 2017

It is confirmed that six White House staff members, including Chief Digital Officer Gerrit Lansing, were removed from their positions earlier in the

month after failing FBI background checks

....

February 24, 2017

The New York Times is barred from the White House press briefing along with the *BBC, CNN, Politico, The Huffington Post, The Los Angeles Times* and *BuzzFeed News*, prompting criticism from the White House Correspondents' Association.

....

February 25, 2017

President Trump becomes the first sitting president to skip the White House Correspondents' Dinner since 1981, when Ronald Reagan was recovering from an assassination attempt.

....

February 27, 2017

Former President George W. Bush offers criticism of the Trump administration's handling of the free press and religious freedom on the TODAY show.

....

February 28, 2017

President Trump signs a bill removing restrictions on the purchase of guns by persons with mental illnesses.

....

February 28, 2017

To stop leaks, the White House approves a rule allowing the staff's cell phones to be searched

....

TRUMP: *Worst. President. Ever.*

2017

March 3, 2017

The White House hires three former lobbyists in agencies they had lobbied against, in violation of President Trump's own ethics rules. An ethics course for new White House staff is eliminated.

March 4, 2017

President Trump publicly accuses former President Obama of intercepting communications at his offices in New York City's Trump Tower in October 2016. This is dismissed as a complete lie.

March 7, 2017

President Trump supports a bill that would repeal the Affordable Care Act and leave 21 million without health insurance according to the Congressional Budget Office.

March 9, 2017

Trump-appointed EPA administrator Scott Pruitt says he does not believe that carbon dioxide was a primary contributor to global warming.

March 9, 2017

Office of Government Ethics demands reprimands for Kellyanne Conway for advertising Ivanka Trump's products on television, but the White House refuses.

March 10, 2017

Former Trump campaign adviser Roger Stone acknowledges personal communication he had with Democratic National Committee hacker Guccifer 2.0.

March 15, 2017

Ambassador to the United Nations Nikki Haley describes the idea of a Muslim ban as "un-American".

March 17, 2017

Britain's Government Communications Headquarters (GCHQ) denies all involvement in the alleged wiretapping of Trump Tower, prompting the Trump administration to issue a formal apology to the United Kingdom with assurances that the allegation will not be repeated.

March 28, 2017

President Trump signs Executive Order 13783, which removes a directive to consider climate change during deliberations under the National Environmental Policy Act, removes restrictions on fracking, and directs the Environmental Protection Agency to suspend, revise or abolish the Clean Power Plan.

TRUMP: *Worst. President. Ever.*

March 28, 2017

The President signs a bill ending the Fair Pay and Safe Workplaces regulation.

March 30, 2017

President Trump calls FBI Director James Comey, asserts that he wasn't involved with Russian hookers and asks Comey to "lift the cloud" of the Russia investigation.

March 30, 2017

Vice President Pence casts his second tie-breaking vote, voting to advance a bill to defund Planned Parenthood.

March 31, 2017

Tom Price, the Secretary of Health and Human Services, purchases 90,000 dollars worth of pharmaceutical stocks a month before the signing of a bill which benefits them.

April 2, 2017

A federal judge rules that before the presidency Trump may have incited violence at a rally in 2016 in Kentucky.

April 3, 2017

President Trump signs a congressional resolution allowing Internet service providers to collect and sell their customers' online usage history with greater ease.

April 7, 2017

The Department of Homeland Security orders Twitter to reveal the identity of a user after their account had been critical of the President and was suspected of working for the government.

April 11, 2017

Press Secretary Spicer makes a televised apology following controversial remarks made at a White House press briefing concerning Adolf Hitler and the use of chemical weaponsuspected of working for the government.

April 11, 2017

The President asks FBI Director James Comey to announce that the Bureau was not investigating him.uspected of working for the government. Comey declines to do so.

April 12, 2017

The Education Secretary Betsy DeVos rolls back student debt repayment protections.

April 14, 2017

The Trump administration verifies that it will discontinue the practice of voluntarily releasing the White House visitors' log

April 15, 2017

Tax Day March rallies are held throughout the U.S. President Trump responds the following day in two tweets, saying "the election is over." Furthermore, Trump claims that protests against him were paid for.

April 17, 2017

President Trump calls leader of Turkey Recep Tayyip Erdoğan to congratulate his victory in a referendum increasing his powers, despite the State Department questioning the democratic legitimacy of the polls that protests against him were paid for.

April 20, 2017

The President's lawyers argue that protesters at his rallies had "no rights" to "express dissenting views" because their First Amendment rights did not apply "as part of the campaign rally of the political candidates they oppose".

April 23, 2017

In response to polls showing the lowest approval rating of any president since 1945, President Trump blames "fake news".

April 24, 2017

The Anti-Defamation League reports an 86% rise in anti-Semitic attacks since the president's inauguration.

April 25, 2017

The president publicly suggests breaking up the United States Court of Appeals for the Ninth Circuit after it block his defunding of sanctuary cities.tacks since the president's inauguration.

April 28, 2017

At the Georgia World Congress Center in Atlanta, President Trump delivers the first presidential address to the National Rifle Association since 1983, reiterating his guarantee of the Second Amendment..tacks since the president's inauguration.

April 28, 2017

The EPA removes all references to climate change from their website..tacks since the president's inauguration.

April 29, 2017

The president falsely claims that the new Republican health care bill would protect health insurance for those with pre-existing conditions.

May 1, 2017

The White House defunds Let Girls Learn, a program initiated by former First Lady Michelle Obama.r those with pre-existing conditions.

May 1, 2017

The Department of Agriculture abandons Obama-era standards for healthier school lunches.a.r those with pre-existing conditions.

May 2, 2017

The Department of Agriculture abandons Obama-era standards for healthier school lunches.

May 2, 2017

The president appoints Teresa Manning, an anti-abortion activist, in charge of family planning for low-income people.

May 8, 2017

The EPA fires half the scientists on its advisory board.

May 9, 2017

President Trump fires James Comey from his position as FBI Director. nstein[190] and Attorney General Sessions, citing Comey's public statements about the Clinton email investigation as the reason for the decision.

May 9, 2017

Journalist Dan Heyman is arrested after questioning Secretary of Health and Human Services Tom Price.

May 17, 2017

President Trump delivers the commencement address at the Coast Guard Academy in New London, Connecticut, with a speech on the theme of persistence, claiming that "No politician—and I say this with great surety—has been treated worse or more unfairly."

May 19, 2017

The White House does not dispute reports that President Trump called former FBI Director Comey a "nut job" and said that firing him "relieved pressure" in a meeting with Russian officials.

May 19, 2017

There are still 700 unfilled positions at the Centers for Disease Control and Prevention

May 20, 2017

President Trump is received in Riyadh by Salman bin Abdulaziz Al Saud and is awarded Saudi Arabia's highest civilian honor, the Collar of Abdulaziz Al Saud. Incidentally, Trump signs an arms deal worth more than $350 billion and various

2017

other investment agreements with Saudi Arabia.

May 21, 2017

The president suggests cutting US$1.7 trillion from redistributive programs such as food stamps and Medicaid.

May 22, 2017

Health insurance providers have raised premiums by up to 50% due to uncertainty surrounding the administration's stance towards the Affordable Care Act.

May 23, 2017

The White House publishes President Trump's first full budget proposal. Allocations include $1.6 billion for a Mexican border wall and a 10% increase in military spending. Reductions include an $800 billion cut to Medicaid, a $190 billion cut to food stamps, cuts to Meals on Wheels and drug treatment programs, and the elimination of student loan subsidies.

May 24, 2017

Secretary of Housing and Urban development Ben Carson calls poverty "a state of mind".

May 25, 2017

During a NATO meeting, the president visibly pushes the Montenegrin Prime Minister Duško Marković out of the way during a photo-op.

May 26, 2017

President Trump attends the 43rd G7 summit. Trump refuses to commit the U.S. to the Paris Agreement on climate change and cutting greenhouse emissions.

May 30, 2017

The White House grants ethics waivers to 17 senior officials.

June 1, 2017

President Trump formally announces his intent to withdraw the U.S. from the 2015 Paris climate agreement, prompting criticism from former and serving world leaders and the United Nations. Tesla's Elon Musk and Disney CEO Bob Iger resign from the president's business advisory council in protest

June 5, 2017

The American ambassador to China resigns in response to the country leaving the Paris Agreement.

June 6, 2017

Press Secretary Spicer confirms that President Trump's tweets are to be "considered official statements by the

TRUMP: *Worst. President. Ever.*

President of the United States".

The White House tries to lessen the severity of a sanctions bill on Russia.

June 12, 2017

President Trump hosts the NCAA champions Clemson Tigers at the White House. He serves them fast food hamburgers.

June 19, 2017

Secretary of Energy Rick Perry says he does not believe carbon dioxide to be causing climate change.

June 12, 2017

The Attorneys General of Maryland and the District of Columbia file a lawsuit against President Trump, alleging violation of the emoluments clause.

June 20, 2017

The Trump administration plans to cut EPA's budget by 31%, firing over 1,200 staff members.

June 22, 2017

Two senior intelligence officials confirm to Robert Mueller that the president had asked them both to publicly announce that he had not colluded with Russia.

June 13, 2017

It is reported that 70% of Trump Organisation properties sold since the election have been to anonymous LLC's, while before the election the figure was 2%.

June 23, 2017

President Trump cuts $400,000 of funding from Life After Hate, a non-profit group which helps people leave the Ku Klux Klan and other white-supremacist and Nazi organizations.

June 15, 2017

The president appoints Eric Trump's wedding planner to run federal housing in New York.

June 27, 2017

The EPA rolls back regulations on drinking water purity.

June 16, 2017

The administration partially rolls back the thawing of ties with Cuba.

June 28, 2017

President Trump holds a 2020 election campaign fundraising event at Trump

June 16, 2017

International Hotel, Washington D.C.

....

June 29, 2017

The president insults MSNBC host Mika Brzezinski, saying she had been "bleeding badly from a face-lift."

....

June 30, 2017

Joe Scarborough and Mika Brzezinski, MSNBC news hosts, state that the White House had blackmailed with an article about their relationship in the *National Enquirer*, demanding they change their news coverage of him.

....

June 30, 2017

President Trump reiterates a prior suggestion to repeal the Affordable Care Act immediately, and replace it later.

....

July 1, 2017

President Trump highlights on Twitter the refusal of 25 states to submit some or all requested voter information to the Presidential Advisory Commission on Election Integrity.

....

July 4, 2017

The number of U.S. states refusing to comply with President Trump's Commission on Election Integrity is reported to have risen to 44.

....

July 8, 2017

First Daughter Ivanka Trump takes President Trump's seat at the G20 summit, drawing rebuke from Chelsea Clinton and Congressional leaders.

....

July 8, 2017

The New York Times reports the existence of a June 9, 2016, meeting between Jared Kushner, Paul Manafort, Donald Trump Jr. and Natalia Veselnitskaya, a Russian attorney. President Trump says the meeting concerned adoption.

....

July 9, 2017

The New York Times reports that Donald Trump Jr. "was promised damaging information about Hillary Clinton before agreeing to meet with a Kremlin-connected Russian lawyer during the 2016 campaign."

....

July 13, 2017

President Trump and First Lady Melania Trump arrive in Paris for a two-day state visit. During the visit the president comments that French first lady Brigitte Macron is "in such good shape".

....

July 19, 2017

The US military is reported to have rented 2.4 million dollars worth of space at the Trump Tower.

....

TRUMP: *Worst. President. Ever.*

July 19, 2017

The president says that he would not have hired Jeff Sessions as the Attorney General if he had known he would recuse himself from the Russia investigation.

....

July 20, 2017

President Trump meets with his national security team at the Pentagon to discuss troop levels in Afghanistan and the fight against the Islamic State of Iraq and the Levant. The meeting is reportedly contentious and became the moment when Secretary of State Rex Tillerson decided to resign his position.

....

July 21, 2017

President Trump appoints Anthony Scaramucci his new White House Communications Director.

....

July 21, 2017

White House Press Secretary Sean Spicer resigns, effective at the end of August.

....

July 21, 2017

H. R. McMaster dismisses Rich Higgins from the National Security Council following exposure of a memorandum, authored by Higgins, outlining a theory that the media, bankers, Islamists, cultural Marxists, and both political parties are plotting to destroy Trump's presidency.

....

July 22, 2017

In a phone call to Ryan Lizza, a *New Yorker* journalist, the newly appointed Communications Director Anthony Scaramucci calls Chief of Staff Reince Priebus a "fucking paranoid schizophrenic" and notes that unlike Steve Bannon he is "not trying to suck my own cock". In 2017, Lizza was fired from *The New Yorker* in relation to an allegation of sexual harassment.

....

July 24, 2017

President Trump attends the 2017 National Scout Jamboree at Glen Jean, West Virginia, praising the organization and its values. The Boy Scouts' chief executive issues a formal apology on July 27 for the speech's "political rhetoric".

....

July 26, 2017

President Trump says, "The United States Government will not accept or allow ... transgender individuals to serve in any capacity in the U.S. Military," citing disruptions and medical costs.

....

July 26, 2017

The Trump administration begins to roll back a regulation expanding overtime pay to 4.2 million workers.

....

TRUMP: *Worst. President. Ever.*

2017

July 26, 2017

The Justice Department files a legal brief on behalf of the United States arguing that the 1964 Civil Rights Act does not prohibit discrimination based on sexual orientation or, implicitly, gender identity.

July 27, 2017

Chief of Staff Reince Priebus resigns.

July 29, 2017

President Trump describes Republican Senators as looking like "fools" following a 49–51 vote against his initiative to repeal the Affordable Care Act.

July 31, 2017

Anthony Scaramucci is removed as the White House Communications Director 16 days after taking office, following crude remarks made in an interview to *The New Yorker.*

July 31, 2017

Press Secretary Sarah Sanders states her belief that President Trump was "joking", when asked about allegations that he promoted police brutality at a speech to law enforcement officers at Suffolk County Community College on July 28.

August 2, 2017

The president is reported to have complained about NATO allies and asked how the US could exploit Afghanistan's mineral wealth.

August 4, 2017

Attorney General Jeff Sessions announces a crackdown on individuals who leak classified or sensitive national security information, as well as a review of the way in which journalists are subpoenaed.

August 9, 2017

President Trump speaks by telephone with Senator Mitch McConnell; he complains that McConnell is not protecting him from the Senate's Russia inquiry.

August 10, 2017

President Trump states that he is "very thankful" that Vladimir Putin ordered removal of 755 diplomatic posts from Russia, reducing the U.S. payroll.

August 11, 2017

President Trump retracts his statement thanking Vladimir Putin on August 10 and states that his original comment was sarcastic.t at Trump International Hotel, Washington D.C.

August 12, 2017

President Trump condemns the violence

TRUMP: *Worst. President. Ever.*

from all sides at a far-right rally at Charlottesville, Virginia, and calls for law and order to be restored. He notably opted to omit any mention of the murdered counter-protester Heather Heyer in his address; he also chose to not single out or specifically condemn the alt-right protester James Alex Fields for that murder, and to not condemn the neo-Nazi movement. Trump faced bipartisan criticism for these omissions.

August 13, 2017

National Security Advisor McMaster denounces a fatal vehicular attack on counterprotestors in Charlottesville on August 12 as "terrorism".

August 14, 2017

Attorney General Sessions decries the August 12 Charlottesville vehicle attack as "domestic terrorism".

August 14, 2017

The CEOs of Merck, Intel and Under Armour resign from the American Manufacturing Council in protest at President Trump's response to the Charlottesville rally.

August 15, 2017

President Trump holds a press conference at which he goes "off teleprompter" and reverts to his earlier apportioning of blame in Charlottesville, apparently equally, to both sides. At this same news conference he voices his personal support of the rationale of the Alt-right's claim that General Lee was a historical figure of similar historical importance to Lincoln, Washington and Jefferson, and that he therefore supported the Alt-Right's rationale for protesting against the removal of the Charlottesville statue of General Lee.

August 15, 2017

Scott Paul, president of the Alliance for American Manufacturing, and Richard Trumka, president of AFL-CIO, resign from the American Manufacturing Council. President Trump describes the resignees as "grandstanders".

August 16, 2017

After the fallout from Trump's handling of the Charlottesville protest, numerous members of President Trump's American Manufacturing Council announce their intention to resign from the Council. President Trump announces the dissolution of the Council and also of the Strategic and Policy Forum following the resignations of Inge Thulin, CEO of 3M, and Campbell's Soup Company CEO Denise Morrison.

August 17, 2017

In an interview with Reuters, President Trump says "I loved my previous life. I had so many things going. This is more work than in my previous life. I thought it would be easier."

TRUMP: *Worst. President. Ever.*

25

2017

August 18, 2017

The White House announces that Chief Strategist Steve Bannon has left his position "by mutual agreement".

August 21, 2017

Seven members of the National Infrastructure Advisory Council send a letter of resignation to the White House, asserting that President Trump is paying "insufficient attention" to cyber-security threats to the nation's infrastructure.

August 22, 2017

Trump announces a willingness to shut down the federal government if Congress refuses to allocate funds for his Mexican wall policy.

August 25, 2017

President Trump issues a presidential pardon for Sheriff Joe Arpaio who was convicted of criminal contempt in a case involving his department's racial profiling policy, praising Arpaio's life work in protecting the public from crime and illegal immigration.

September 2, 2017

Press Secretary Sanders denies a report that Director of Oval Office Operations Keith Schiller intends to resign.

September 7, 2017

The Trump Justice Department files a legal brief in the Supreme Court, arguing for a constitutional right of businesses to discriminate on the basis of sexual orientation and, implicitly, gender identity.

September 19, 2017

In his maiden speech to the United Nations General Assembly, President Trump announces that if Kim Jong-un, dubbed "Rocket Man", forces the United States to defend itself or its allies, the United States will "totally destroy" North Korea. Trump also indicates the possibility of further action against Venezuelan President Maduro's regime, denounces Iran as a "corrupt dictatorship", and describes the Iranian nuclear deal as an "embarrassment". He calls on the UN to work together to solve such issues.

September 20, 2017

Long-time aide and confidant to President Trump Keith Schiller leaves his position as the Director of Oval Office Operations.

September 21, 2017

The White House instructs the Environment Protection Agency to

TRUMP: *Worst. President. Ever.*

begin ordering employees to attend anti-leaking class to reinforce their compliance with laws and rules against leaking classified or sensitive government information to the media or outside parties.

September 22, 2017

Secretary of Education Betsy DeVos rescinds the previous administration's guidelines for colleges and universities in handling sexual misconduct claims under Title IX and introduced new guidelines in reporting these claims.

September 23, 2017

In response to a tweet by President Trump withdrawing an invitation to NBA player Stephen Curry to visit the White House, the entire Golden State Warrior team says it will forego the traditional championship team Oval office visit.

September 26, 2017

A third attempt at a Senate vote on President Trump's initiative to repeal the Affordable Care Act is abandoned.

September 28, 2017

It is reported that the White House is conducting an investigation into the use of private email accounts by senior members of the administration, including Jared Kushner, for official business.

September 29, 2017

Secretary of Health and Human Services Tom Price resigns from his position after reports of criticism over extensive use of private jets.

October 1, 2017

The deadline passes unfulfilled for President Trump to identify for punishment Kremlin-linked targets of sanctions signed on August 2.

October 4, 2017

UN Ambassador Nikki Haley has been formally reprimanded for violating the Hatch Act.

October 8, 2017

At President Trump's prior request, Vice President Pence walks out of an NFL football game after fifteen 49er players kneel during the national anthem.

October 12, 2017

The Trump administration announces that the U.S. will withdraw from UNESCO, citing an "anti-Israel bias".

October 13, 2017

President Trump attends the Values Voter Summit in Washington D.C. to speak on matters such as easing of enforcement of the Johnson Amendment, a provision in the U.S. tax code, since 1954, that

TRUMP: *Worst. President. Ever.*

prohibits all 501(c)(3) non-profit organizations from endorsing or opposing political candidates, and weakening the contraception mandate in the Affordable Care Act.

....

October 15, 2017

President Trump's 2020 re-election campaign files its quarterly finance report with the FEC. The filing discloses a legal bill of $1.1m paid from campaign funds in connection with the Russia investigations.

....

October 16, 2017

Responding to questions at the White House, President Trump makes his first public comments on the four Special Forces soldiers killed in a suspected ISIS ambush on October 4 and slams President Obama's contacting of slain soldier's families.

....

October 17, 2017

Trump's nominee to lead the White House Office of National Drug Control Policy, Tom Marino, withdraws his nomination following news reports that Marino had previously worked on behalf of the pharmaceutical industry.

....

October 18, 2017

The latest version of President Trump's travel ban is blocked by U.S. District Judge Derrick Watson shortly before it comes into effect.

....

October 18, 2017

President Trump meets with Puerto Rico Governor Ricardo Rosselló at the White House to discuss the island's recovery efforts after Hurricane Maria, after he initially suggested Hurricane Maria wasn't "a real catastrophe."

....

October 24, 2017

President Trump holds a swearing-in ceremony at the Oval Office for the next Ambassador to the Vatican Callista Gingrich, who married the former Speaker of the House Newt Gingrich after an affair and annulment of his previous 20-year marriage.

....

October 26, 2017

President Trump signs a presidential memorandum declaring a nationwide public health emergency and ordering all federal agencies to take measures to reduce the number of opioid deaths in the country. No funds are allocated from the public health emergency fund.

....

October 30, 2017

Shortly following the surrender of former Trump campaign officials Paul Manafort and Rick Gates to the FBI on twelve charges of conspiracy and money laundering between 2006 and 2015, President Trump states on Twitter that

TRUMP: *Worst. President. Ever.*

the charges refer to events from "years ago".

....

October 30, 2017

Following the announcement of a guilty plea from George Papadopolous concerning lying to the FBI about meetings with Russians in 2016, Press Secretary Sanders describes Papadopoulos having held a 'limited', 'volunteer' position in the Trump campaign. Sanders contradicts Mueller's indictment which details that Papadopoulos was encouraged to meet with Russian officials by a high-ranking Trump campaign official. President Trump describes former foreign policy aide George Papadopoulos as a "young, low level volunteer" and a "liar".

....

October 30, 2017

The enforcement of President Trump's ban on transgender soldiers is blocked by U.S. District Judge Colleen Kollar-Kotelly, stating that the President's given reasons "do not appear to be supported by any facts".

....

November 7, 2017

President Trump tweets his support for Republican candidate Ed Gillespie and attacks Democratic candidate Ralph Northam in advance of the election of a new Governor of Virginia. Northam wins.

....

November 9, 2017

The State Department rejects an essay released by Ambassador Barbara Stephenson, which claims that the continuing depletion of State officials under the Trump administration will "forfeit the game to our adversaries".

....

November 14, 2017

Attorney General Jeff Sessions testifies to the House Judiciary Committee. He states that he now recalls learning of contact between Russians and the Trump campaign, but denies previously lying under oath.

....

November 14, 2017

Attorney General Jeff Sessions says he has no reason to disbelieve those who accuse Republican Senate candidate Roy Moore of sexual activity with young girls, whom Trump has endorsed.

....

November 16, 2017

Senators Chuck Grassley and Dianne Feinstein disclose that presidential advisor Jared Kushner has failed to submit to them numerous documents concerning Wikileaks and "a Russian backdoor overture".

....

November 20, 2017

President Trump announces that North Korea will be reinstated to the United States' list of State Sponsors of Terrorism, from which it was removed in October 2008.

....

TRUMP: *Worst. President. Ever.*

November 21, 2017

President Trump defends Senate candidate Roy Moore from accusations of sex abuse.

November 27, 2017

President Trump hosts a White House event honoring Second World War Navajo code talker veterans. The White House later states that it is 'ridiculous' to suggest that Trump's reiteration at the event of the name 'Pocahontas' to describe Senator Elizabeth Warren is racist, following protestation by the National Congress of American Indians and others.

November 27, 2017

Politico reports that White House ethics lawyer James Schultz has recently resigned.

November 29, 2017

President Trump retweets anti-Muslim propaganda posted by the convicted criminal Jayda Fransen, deputy leader of British far-right organization Britain First. British Prime Minister May condemns the action. Trump's plan to visit the UK in the New Year is abandoned on the following day.

November 30, 2017

Press Secretary Sanders denies reports that Secretary Rex Tillerson is to be fired.

November 30, 2017

Jeff Sessions testifies at a private meeting of the House Intelligence Committee. According to ranking member Schiff, Sessions refuses to say whether or not President Trump asked him to hinder the Russia investigation.

December 1, 2017

Former Trump National Security Advisor Michael Flynn pleads guilty to lying to the FBI on January 24, 2017, concerning contacts with Russian Ambassador Sergey Kislyak.

December 3, 2017

President Trump's lawyer John M. Dowd states that Trump knew in January 2017 that Michael Flynn had lied to the FBI.

December 3, 2017

Ambassador Nikki Haley informs UN Secretary-General António Guterres that the U.S. is to remove itself from the UN's 2016 New York declaration for refugees and migrants.

December 4, 2017

TRUMP: *Worst. President. Ever.*

President Trump announces 85% and 50% reductions respectively to Utah's Bears Ears National Monument and Grand Staircase-Escalante National Monument. The monument's reduction was seen as a victory for Republican officials and energy companies with mining leases for fossil fuel and uranium deposits.

....

December 4, 2017

President Trump formally endorses Senate candidate Roy Moore, accused of sexual assault on minors.

....

December 5, 2017

Press Secretary Sanders denies that President Trump is planning to create his own private global spy network. This is contradicted by a current U.S. intelligence official, stating that the various proposals were first pitched at the White House before being delivered to the CIA.

....

December 6, 2017

President Trump announces that the United States is to recognize Jerusalem as the capital of Israel—the first nation to do so—and announces that the U.S. will relocate its embassy there from Tel Aviv.

....

December 10, 2017

Palestinian President Mahmoud Abbas refuses to meet with Vice President Pence. Pence's office describes the decision as "unfortunate".

....

December 11, 2017

President Trump signs a policy directive at the White House, ordering NASA to reprioritize manned voyages, including a return to the Moon and a mission to Mars. The U.S. was last on the moon 45 years ago.

....

December 12, 2017

President Trump signs the National Defense Authorization Act's 2018 budget, costed at $700 billion. It provides $25m for road-based cruise missile technology, in violation of the 1987 and 1988 Intermediate-Range Nuclear Forces Treaty.

....

December 12, 2017

President Trump tweets his support for Republican candidate Roy Moore and condemns Democratic candidate Doug Jones on the day of Alabama's special Senate election to fill the seat vacated by Jeff Sessions in February 2017. Jones wins.

....

December 13, 2017

Director of Communications for the White House's Office of Public Liaison, Omarosa Manigault, is to resign on January 20, 2018. Reports are that Manigault, whose previous experience was on the Trump-hosted show *The*

TRUMP: *Worst. President. Ever.*   31

Apprentice, was fired by Chief of Staff John Kelly and had to be physically removed from the White House grounds.

December 14, 2017

A seventh U.S. Senator, Kamala Harris (in addition to Kirsten Gillibrand, Bernie Sanders, Cory Booker, Ron Wyden, Mazie Hirono, Jeff Merkley) calls on Trump to resign, due to the credible allegations of sexual assault against him by 19 women.

December 15, 2017

Speaking at the White House, President Trump describes the FBI as acting disgracefully and states that people are angry. Trump shortly thereafter addresses a group of largely non-FBI graduates from a program at the FBI National Academy in Quantico, Virginia, stating "I have your back 100%".

December 16, 2017

The U.S. blocks a resolution by the other 14 members of the UN Security Council calling for a retraction of President Trump's recent statement recognizing Jerusalem as Israel's capital. Ambassador Haley describes the resolution as an insult which "won't be forgotten".

December 19, 2017

Ambassador Haley states that she will be "taking names" of countries who vote in favor of the December 21 UN resolution against U.S. recognition of Jerusalem as Israel's capital and passing them to President Trump, who has suggested cutting aid to countries who do so.

December 20, 2017

The Senate passes President Trump's Tax Cuts and Jobs Act shortly after midnight without Democratic votes, 51 to 48. The wide-ranging bill includes a cut to corporate tax from 35% to 21%, a reduction to the pool of estate-tax payers, alters each tax bracket, and reduces the rate for the highest earners. The bill also permits oil drilling in Alaska's Arctic National Wildlife Refuge and removes the individual mandate from Obamacare. President Trump announces that the bill represents a repeal of Obamacare, and that it will be replaced by "something that will be much better". The legislation is financed by debt.

December 21, 2017

The United Nations votes 128 to 9 in favor of a demand that the U.S. retract its recent declaration concerning Jerusalem. U.S. Ambassador Haley describes the vote as 'null and void'.

December 27, 2017

All ten members of the Presidential Advisory Council on HIV/AIDS are dismissed.

December 29, 2017

Trump's Labor Department continues the policy of issuing waivers to banks convicted of manipulating the global interest rate Libor. Deutsche Bank and UBS are allowed to manage retirement funds for three years. At the time, Trump and his businesses owe Deutsche Bank at least $130 million.

January 2, 2018

President Trump tweets that his "nuclear button" is larger and more powerful than that of Kim Jong-un.

January 2, 2018

President Trump threatens to cut off U.S. aid to the Palestinian Authority, claiming the Palestinians were no longer willing to negotiate on a peace process with the Israelis—seemingly after his December 2017 decision to recognize Jerusalem as the capital of Israel.

January 2, 2018

President Trump disbands his Presidential Advisory Commission on Election Integrity. The commission was charged with protecting the electrion process from fraud.

January 3, 2018

President Trump issues a

statement describing Steve Bannon, former CEO of the Trump campaign, as having "very little to do with our historic victory" and as having "lost his mind".

January 4, 2018

President Trump's lawyer Charles J. Harder sends to Michael Wolff and his publisher, Henry Holt and Company, a cease and desist letter demanding the non-publication of Wolff's White House exposé, *Fire and Fury*, due for release on January 9. Wolff's publishers move the date of publication forward to January 5.

January 4, 2018

Secretary of the Interior Ryan Zinke announces a plan to open up 90% of the U.S. coastline to oil drilling.

January 6, 2018

President Trump tweets that he is a "very stable genius", praising his own "mental stability". Also within the tweet, he says he became president "on the first try", despite having run as a Reform Party candidate in 2000.

January 9, 2018

District judge William Alsup rules that

the DACA program must remain in place while litigation continues over the Trump administration's September 5 decision to end it. The next morning, Trump describes the U.S. court system as "broken and unfair".

January 9, 2018

Secretary Zinke announces that Florida, a key electoral college state, will be exempted from oil drilling under the new policy announced on January 4.

January 10, 2018

President Trump reiterates that he will be reviewing libel law, describing the current law as "a sham and a disgrace". This follows as a result of the publication of Michael Wolff's *Fire and Fury*.

January 11, 2018

The Trump administration announces new state guidelines that Medicaid recipients will be required to work or volunteer, or enroll in education, regardless of physical condition.

January 11, 2018

President Trump, in a meeting with Senators Lindsey Graham (R-SC) and Dick Durbin (D-IL) regarding immigration law reform, referred to Haiti and African countries as "shithole countries" and expressed preference for immigrants from Norway.

January 12, 2018

President Trump cancels a planned visit to the UK, blaming his predecessor, Barack Obama, for a "bad deal" on the new embassy due to be opened in London, despite the fact it was agreed under George W. Bush.

January 12, 2018

Citing disagreements with the Trump administration, John Feeley announces his resignation as U.S. Ambassador to Panama. Panama will join the dozens of countries that do not currently have Senate-confirmed US ambassadors in place, including key US allies like South Korea, Jordan and Saudi Arabia.

January 15, 2018

The Wall Street Journal reports that Jared Kushner was warned in early 2017 by U.S. intelligence officials that his friend Wendi Deng Murdoch may be a Chinese spy. Mrs. Murdoch is the third wife of Fox News head Rupert Murdoch.

January 17, 2018

In Touch Weekly publishes excerpts from a 2011 interview with adult-film actress Stormy Daniels alleging a 2006 extramarital affair with Trump. The magazine describes her passing a polygraph and her friend's and ex-husband's both corroborating the interview. Trump was newly married at the time to his pregnant wife, Melania.

....

January 18, 2018

Hungarian police have an active arrest warrant, issued on September 17, 2016, against former Trump White House advisor Sebastian Gorka. The warrant concerns alleged abuse of firearms.

....

January 19, 2018

German periodical *Manager Magazin* reports that Deutsche Bank has presented to Germany's financial authority, BaFin, evidence concerning "suspicious money transfers" by White House advisor Jared Kushner. MM reports that this information is due to be handed to Robert Mueller's inquiry.

....

January 20, 2018

A federal government shutdown begins, after the Senate fails to pass a continuing resolution to maintain funding for the government. Trump celebrates one year in office.

....

January 21, 2018

Vice President Pence meets with King Abdullah II of Jordan in Amman. Abdullah criticizes the decision to recognize Jerusalem as the Israeli capital.

....

January 22, 2018

During the third day of the federal government shutdown, President Trump accuses the Democratic Party of precipitating the shutdown "in the interests of their far left base".

....

January 25, 2018

The New York Times reports that President Trump ordered the dismissal of the special counsel, Robert Mueller, in June 2017, but retreated upon the threatened resignation of White House counsel Don McGahn; this elevated concerns of possible obstruction of justice.

....

January 29, 2018

Deputy FBI Director Andrew McCabe resigns from his position, but remained as part of the FBI, after criticism from President Trump in preceding weeks.

....

January 30, 2018

The White House confirms that President Trump has signed an order keeping open the Guantanamo Bay detention camp in Cuba.

....

January 31, 2018

The White House confirms that President Trump has signed an order keeping open the Guantanamo Bay detention camp in Cuba.

....

January 31, 2018

Doctor Brenda Fitzgerald resigns as Director of the

Center for Disease Control over conflicts of interest. Fitzgerald bought shares in Japan Tobacco one month into her leadership of the agency, which is responsible for reducing tobacco use among Americans.

February 5, 2018

At a speech in Cincinnati, Ohio, President Trump claims that Congressional Democrats, who "were like death and un-American" in not applauding during his State of the Union speech, were "treasonous" and that "we call that treason".

February 6, 2018

While Congress was preparing a continuing resolution for a temporary budget, President Trump declared, "I'd love to see a shutdown" if American immigration laws were not tightened. He also said "it's worth it for our country".

February 7, 2018

White House Staff Secretary Rob Porter resigns from his position following two public allegations of spousal abuse.

February 12, 2018

President Trump sends his $4.4 trillion 2019 budget proposal to Congress. Trump's budget would add $7 trillion to deficits.

February 16, 2018

The New Yorker reports that President Trump had a nine-month extramarital affair with Playboy model Karen McDougal from June 2006, citing handwritten memoirs by McDougal provided by her friend.

February 28, 2018

A day after being interviewed by the U.S. House Intelligence Committee, White House Communications Director Hope Hicks submits her resignation.

March 1, 2018

Two-time NBA champions Golden State Warriors snub Trump and toured the National Museum of African American History and Culture as an alternative to the traditional White House visit.

March 1, 2018

The U.S. Fish and Wildlife Service removes the blanket ban on imports of sport-hunted trophies of elephants from certain African countries originally imposed by the Obama administration. The organization also withdrew several Endangered Species Act findings regarding African elephants, lions and the bontebok antelopes.

March 1, 2018

Roberta Jacobson, the Ambassador to Mexico, resigns from her post, citing relations with Trump.

....

March 3, 2018

In a speech to Republican donors at Mar-a-Lago, President Trump says "it's great" that Chinese President Xi Jinping was able to become "president for life", and that "maybe we'll have to give that a shot some day."

....

March 6, 2018

The U.S. Office of Special Counsel (OSC) says Counselor to the President Kellyanne Conway violated federal law in the form of the Hatch Act during two television interviews in 2017 by advocating for the defeat of Doug Jones and the election of Roy Moore for Alabama's election for a Senate seat.

....

March 6, 2018

Chief economic adviser Gary Cohn announces plan to resign after President Trump announced he would impose tariffs on steel and aluminum imports.

....

March 7, 2018

U.S. Forest Service Chief Tom Tooke resigns from his post, amid a sexual misconduct investigation against him. He is replaced by Vicki Christiansen, the first firefighter to be Chief of the U.S. Forest Service, the agency in charge of fire protection of federal lands.

....

March 8, 2018

President Trump meets with video-game executives to discuss how violent video games might contribute to mass shootings. The CDC states there is no link between video games and gun violence.

....

March 10, 2018

President Trump holds a rally at the Pittsburgh International Airport to support Rick Saccone in an upcoming special election. He introduces his 2020 campaign slogan: "Keep America Great!"

....

March 13, 2018

President Trump fires Rex Tillerson as Secretary of State, names former CIA director Mike Pompeo as the new Secretary of State, and nominates Gina Haspel as the next director of the CIA.

....

March 13, 2018

John McEntee, a long-time personal assistant to President Trump, is fired after being investigated by the Department of Homeland Security for serious financial crimes, and escorted from the White House.

....

March 16, 2018

TRUMP: *Worst. President. Ever.*

Andrew McCabe, former acting director of the FBI who was due to retire with benefits in two days, was fired from the FBI by Attorney General Jeff Sessions on the recommendation of FBI disciplinary officials for "lack of candor".

March 20, 2018

The Kremlin announces President Trump's call to congratulate Russian President Vladimir Putin on his election victory.[152] National security advisers warned Trump against the call.

March 22, 2018

H.R. McMaster resigns as National Security Adviser and John Bolton, a former ambassador to the United Nations, is named to succeed him.

March 28, 2018

President Trump fires Secretary of Veteran Affairs David Shulkin and nominates White House doctor Ronny L. Jackson to replace him. Shulkin is one of five Trump cabinet officials whose travel practices were scrutinized by internal watchdogs.

April 4, 2018

President Trump signs a proclamation directing the deployment of the National Guard to the U.S.–Mexico border to fight illegal immigration. Troops are forbidden to conduct civilian police actions, such as detaining suspects and using force, under a law first signed by President Rutherford B. Hayes in 1878.

April 9, 2018

After the FBI and federal prosecutors raid the home, hotel room, and office of President Trump's personal attorney, Michael Cohen, Trump brands the raid as "an attack on our country in a true sense".

April 9, 2018

President Trump meets with military leaders to discuss a response to poison gas attacks in Syria. Trump tweets a warning that "an attack on Syria could be very soon or not soon at all!"

April 10, 2018

The White House confirms the resignation of Homeland Security advisor Thomas Bossert and National Security Council spokesman Michael Anton. Nearly 30 White House officials have resigned or been fired under Mr Trump.

April 12, 2018

President Trump launches a task force to "conduct a thorough evaluation of the operations and finances of the United States Postal System". Trump claims Amazon is costing the Postal Service "billions of dollars", although this proven to be false.

April 13, 2018

President Trump pardons Scooter Libby, the former chief of staff for Vice President Dick Cheney in the George W. Bush Administration. As a result of the Plame investigation into the leaking of an undercover CIA agent's identity, Libby had been found guilty of making false statements, obstruction of justice and lying under oath.

April 13, 2018

President Trump sends a series of tweets attacking James Comey, the fired FBI director, as a liar and a "slimeball" and suggests Comey should be in jail.

April 17, 2018

UN Ambassador Nikki Haley responds to a claim by White House economic adviser Larry Kudlow that she was confused when she announced a rollout of sanctions on Russia by commenting, "With all due respect, I don't get confused."

April 19, 2018

Rudy Giuliani, as well as Jane and Marty Raskin, join President Trump's legal team. Giuliani states why he was brought in: "I'm doing it because I hope we can negotiate an end to this (Mueller investigation.)"

April 21, 2018

President Trump uses Twitter to attack New York Times reporter Maggie Haberman following an article she wrote about his poor treatment of Michael Cohen and that Cohen may cooperate with prosecutors as a result.

April 22, 2018

President Trump tweets a claim that North Korea has agreed to denuclearize. Actually, North Korean leader Kim Jong Un released a statement that said "that (nuclear) tests were no longer needed because the country had met its goal of developing its weapons capability.

April 25, 2018

Bryan Rice, director of the Interior Department's Bureau of Indian Affairs, resigned following a claim that he behaved aggressively toward a female employee

April 26, 2018

Dr. Ronny Jackson, Trump's private doctor, withdraws his nomination to head the Department of Veterans Affairs. Jackson was accused of multiple incidents of drunkenness on duty, and nicknamed "Candyman" because he would provide prescriptions without paperwork.

TRUMP: *Worst. President. Ever.*   39

2018

May 4, 2018

Over the preceding week, four EPA officials have resigned: Albert "Kell" Kelly, the top Superfund advisor; Pasquale Perrotta, the head of Administrator Pruitt's security detail; Associate Administrator Liz Bowman; and today John Konkus, deputy Associate Administrator for public affairs.

May 8, 2018

The White House denies a *New York Times* report that President Trump has privately told French President Emmanuel Macron the U.S. is withdrawing from the Iran nuclear deal.

May 8, 2018

President Trump announces in a speech that the U.S. will withdraw from the Iran nuclear deal and reinstate sanctions.

May 9, 2018

R. Timothy Ziemer, the official on the National Security Council responsible for global health security and biodefense against pandemics, is fired and his position is abolished.

May 11, 2018

Kelly Sadler, a White House official, mocks Senator John McCain, saying his opposition to Gina Haspel, Trump's nominee for CIA director, "doesn't matter, he's dying anyway".

May 11, 2018

Emails among U.S. government officials show the Trump administration trying to manage a damaging report on toxic chemicals found to have polluted water supplies near U.S. military installations. Officials warned of a "public relations nightmare" when the report is released.

May 15, 2018

The Trump Administration eliminates the White House's top cyber security policy role and fires Rob Joyce, the coordinator, removing him from the White House.

May 15, 2018

UN Ambassador Nikki Haley walks out of UN Security Council as Palestinian Ambassador Riyad H. Mansour begins his remarks.

May 16, 2018

President Trump submits a disclosure of personal finances which is required by the Office of Government Ethics. Trump acknowledges that Michael Cohen was paid between $100,000 and $250,000 in 2017 for his Stormy Daniels affair.

May 18, 2018

Mark Inch, the director of Federal Prisons, resigns after seven months on the job. The agency has been confronting issues of persistent overcrowding, sub-par inmate medical care, chronic staffing shortages and a lurid sexual harassment lawsuit .

....

May 22, 2018

Reporters from CNN and The Associated Press are denied entry and forcibly removed from the PFAS National Leadership Summit event at the EPA where Scott Pruitt was to speak.

....

May 24, 2018

President Trump cancels the proposed June nuclear summit with North Korea via a letter to Kim Jong-un, after it is revealed that North Korea had not abandoned its nuclear program as Trump had proclaimed.

....

June 1, 2018

President Trump announces that the North Korea–United States summit would resume as scheduled for June 12 in Singapore after he met North Korean general Kim Yong-chol at the White House.

....

June 4, 2018

Raj Shah announces via email that Kelly Sadler, a member of the White House communications staff, is "... no longer employed within the Executive Office of the President". Sadler had previously mocked the dying senator John McCain.

....

June 9, 2018

After President Trump leaves the 44th G7 summit early, he withdraws the United States' endorsement of a joint communique by the G7, and labels Canadian Prime Minister Justin Trudeau "Very dishonest & meek".

....

October 23, 2019

The book All the President's Women: Donald Trump and the Making of a Predator, by Barry Levine and Monique El-Faizy was published, detailing 43 separate allegations of sexual misconduct against Trump.

....

June 10, 2018

Trade adviser Peter Navarro says there is "a special place in hell for" Canadian Prime Minister Justin Trudeau for having employed "bad faith diplomacy with President Donald J. Trump and then tries to stab him in the back on the way out the door ... that comes right from Air Force One." The Trump administration had recently levied tariffs on Canadian aluminum and steel.

....

June 10, 2018

Politico reports that Trump frequently and routinely would tear up papers he received, resulting in government officials' taping them together for archiving to ensure he had not

TRUMP: *Worst. President. Ever.* 41

violated the Presidential Records Act.

June 15, 2018

The Department of Homeland Security states that between April 19 and May 31, 2018, there were 1,995 migrant children separated at the Mexico–United States border from 1,940 adults who are being held for criminal prosecution for an illegal border crossing.

June 15, 2018

President Trump says in response to the situation: "I hate to see separation of parents and children ... I hate the children being taken away." Trump then falsely blames the Democrats for the situation when it was the Trump administration's own "zero tolerance" policy announced on April 6, 2018, which is responsible for spurring the separations.

June 15, 2018

A White House official is quoted as saying that Trump's decision to enforce the current immigration law is "force people to the table" to negotiate on laws in Congress. Meanwhile, Trump tweets: "Any Immigration Bill MUST HAVE full funding for the Wall, end Catch & Release, Visa Lottery and Chain, and go to Merit Based Immigration."

June 15, 2018

Trump falsely claims that a report by Justice Department Inspector General Michael E. Horowitz "totally exonerates" him, despite the report's having nothing to do with the 2017 special counsel investigation, the Trump campaign or Russia. The report was instead focused on the FBI's 2016 investigation of the Hillary Clinton email controversy.

July 5, 2018

Scott Pruitt resigns as EPA Administrator, effective July 6, amidst fifteen federal investigations by various government ethics agencies for his assorted management scandals. Pruitt goes on to promote overseas coal sales for coal baron Joseph Craft III.

July 6, 2018

Andrew Wheeler, a former coal lobbyist and Deputy Administrator of the EPA since April 2018, succeeds Scott Pruitt as acting EPA administrator. The coal industry is recognized as one of the more egregious polluters of the environment.

July 9, 2018

President Trump nominates Brett Kavanaugh, a U.S. Appellate Court Judge on the District of Columbia Circuit, to fill the vacancy on the U.S. Supreme Court created by the impending retirement of Associate Justice Anthony Kennedy. The 81-year-old's announcement was the culmination of a carefully orchestrated

17-month campaign by the Trump administration to remake the Supreme Court

....

July 13, 2018

Special counsel Robert Mueller indicts twelve Russian intelligence officers, alleging that they "engag[ed] in a 'sustained effort' to hack Democrats' emails and computer networks".

....

July 13, 2018

President Trump holds a bilateral meeting and joint press conference with British Prime Minister Theresa May at Chequers. President Trump advises May to "sue the E.U." during Brexit negotiations.

....

July 15, 2018

President Trump remarks during a CBS interview, "Now you wouldn't think of the European Union, but they're a foe," in response to a question about the biggest foes of the United States.

....

July 16, 2018

President Trump and Russian President Vladimir Putin participate in a summit at the Presidential Palace in Helsinki, Finland. At the joint press conference, Trump reiterates both his faulting of "U.S. foolishness and stupidity" and the

Mueller investigation for the freeze in relations between Russia and the United States and his refusal to recognize the Russian government's interference in the 2016 U.S. elections, despite extensive assessments by United States intelligence agencies.

....

July 16, 2018

President Trump receives bi-partisan criticism: prominent Republican senators call his summit performance "disgraceful", "shameful", and "a sign of weakness"; former CIA Director John Brennan calls it "imbecilic" and "nothing short of treasonous".

....

July 17, 2018

The Treasury Department repeals the requirement of some non-profit groups, most prominently the National Rifle Association (NRA), to disclose their donor lists to the Internal Revenue Service. The rule change is announced whilst the NRA was named as the "primary avenue of influence" for Maria Butina, a Russian national charged on July 16 by the national security division of the Justice Department with conspiracy to act as an agent of the Russian government within the United States without the requisite notification to the U.S. Attorney General.

....

July 18, 2018

When asked by a reporter before a Cabinet meeting whether he believes that the Russian government continues to make efforts to interfere in American elections, Trump replied, "no". However,

Sarah Huckabee Sanders (the White House Press Secretary) disputed that Trump was in fact answering the reporter's question when he said "no", and Trump himself refused to clarify his intent to the press later in the day.

....

July 18, 2018

The New York Times reports that Trump was briefed on January 6, 2017, regarding the Russian government's attempts to interfere in American elections. Trump "sounded begrudgingly convinced", according to the Times's sources.

....

July 19, 2018

Trump receives a public request from Russian prosecutors for permission to interrogate eleven American citizens. Trump does not refuse it. After a non-binding resolution to oppose permitting Russian investigators to interrogate any American citizen passes in the United States Senate by a vote of 98–0, the Trump administration issues a statement that the request "was made in sincerity by President Putin, but President Trump disagrees with it".

....

July 19, 2018

Trump invites Russian President Vladimir Putin to Washington, D.C., in the fall, according to a tweet from Sarah Huckabee Sanders.

....

July 19, 2018

Dan Coats (the Director of National Intelligence) reacts to the news of the Putin invitation in a manner deemed by White House officials to be "laughing at the president".

....

July 20, 2018

Trump's long-time lawyer, Michael Cohen, secretly recorded a phone call in which Trump and Cohen discuss a September 2016 payment, in the amount of $150,000, by American Media, Inc. (the owner of the National Enquirer) to Playboy model Karen McDougal in order to acquire the exclusive rights to her story of her 2006 affair with Trump. The National Enquirer never planned on publishing McDougal's story, so the payment (termed a "catch and kill" payment) effectively silenced McDougal's story for the duration of the 2016 presidential campaign. The New York Times also reported that the tape contains a discussion of a back-payment from Trump to American Media, Inc.; the reporting directly contradicted Trump's long-standing claim that he had no knowledge of the payment to either McDougal or American Media, Inc.

....

July 20, 2018

Special counsel Robert Mueller moves to subpoena Kristin Davis, the prostitution mogul known as the "Manhattan Madam". Davis had been best known for her role in the 2008 prostitution scandal involving then-Governor Eliot Spitzer of New York, but she was also a former employee of Roger Stone, a Republican political operative and strategist for Trump.

....

July 22, 2018

Trump tweets that Russian interference in the 2016 U.S. elections is "all a big hoax",[59] appearing to reverse his position yet again on whether the Russian government interfered (and continues to attempt to interfere) in U.S. elections.

....

July 23, 2018

President Trump publicly considers revoking security clearances for former top-level officials (including John Brennan, James Clapper, James Comey, Susan Rice, Andrew McCabe, and Michael Hayden); Trump claims that the former officials' public comments about the Special Counsel investigation are "inappropriate".

....

July 25, 2018

Eleven Republican members of the House Judiciary Committee (all members of the House Freedom Caucus) file an impeachment resolution against Deputy Attorney General Rod Rosenstein, claiming that Rosenstein in his role as overseer of the Special Counsel investigation committed "high crimes and misdemeanors" in refusing to turn over information relating to the ongoing investigation to the House Judiciary Committee.

....

July 26, 2018

The House Republicans who filed an impeachment resolution against Deputy Attorney General Rod Rosenstein on July 26 back down, deciding not to continue with impeachment proceedings. This decision comes after many high-profile Republicans, including House Speaker Paul Ryan and U.S. Attorney General Jeff Sessions, criticize the impeachment resolution and express support for Rosenstein.

....

July 26, 2018

Trump's former lawyer, Michael Cohen, claims that Trump had contemporaneous knowledge of the June 2016 Trump Tower meeting between Trump campaign officials (including Trump's son, Don Jr., and son-in-law, Jared Kushner) and Russian lobbyists, where the Trump campaign was promised "dirt" on Hillary Clinton.

....

July 29, 2018

Trump tweets a threat to support a government shutdown if Democratic lawmakers do not vote for "Border Security, which includes the Wall!"

....

July 30, 2018

After President Trump has claimed "no collusion" for months, his legal adviser Rudy Giuliani says that "I don't even know if [colluding with Russia] is a crime". Another Trump adviser, former Gov. Chris

Christie of New Jersey, echoes the sentiment, saying that "collusion is not a crime".

July 30, 2018

Giuliani also claimed the existence of a previously-unknown June 7, 2016, meeting between Trump campaign officials and Russian lobbyists preceding the Trump Tower meeting on June 9, 2016; however, Giuliani later said that the meeting "never happened".

July 30, 2018

According to U.S. intelligence agencies, North Korea continues to construct nuclear missiles capable of reaching the United States, despite peace talks at the June 12 summit between Trump and Chairman Kim Jong-un.

July 31, 2018

During a rally in Florida, President Trump defends strict "voter ID" laws by claiming that Americans are required to show identification to purchase groceries.

August 1, 2018

President Trump tweets that "Attorney General Jeff Sessions should stop this Rigged Witch Hunt right now, before it continues to stain our country any further", the first time Trump has publicly and explicitly called for the termination of the Special Counsel investigation. Many observers note that this tweet raises concerns about possible obstruction of justice.

August 2, 2018

Sarah Huckabee Sanders (the White House Press Secretary) calls the press the "enemy of the people".

August 2, 2018

At a press conference, top national security officials (Dan Coats, Kirstjen Nielsen, John Bolton, Christopher Wray, and Paul Nakasone) announce that the administration will "make the matter of election meddling and securing our election process a top priority". The officials also affirm that the Russian government is attempting to interfere in the U.S. midterm elections, specifically with "a pervasive messaging campaign by Russia to try to weaken and divide the United States". President Trump falsely claims that there is no Russian interference.

August 3, 2018

A Justice Department filing on a case against the American Civil Liberties Union (ACLU) regarding reunification of separated migrant families argues that it is the responsibility of the plaintiffs (i.e., the ACLU), not the government, to use its "considerable resources" to find parents of separated children whom the government has already deported. The judge who requested the government filing (Dana Sabraw, a U.S. District Court Judge appointed by President George W.

Bush) calls the government's slow pace in reuniting the separated families "unacceptable", and rejects "100%" the argument that the responsibility is on the ACLU to reunite the families.

....

August 9, 2018

The White House director of strategic communications, Mercedes Schlapp, confirms with Univision that Helen Aguirre Ferré, the White House director of media affairs for Latino and African-American news outlets, has resigned from the White House. This is widely seen to be as a result of the Trump-ordered border crisis of family separations.

....

August 12, 2018

Two days before her memoir (Unhinged) is released, Omarosa Manigault, a former White House aide to Trump primarily known for her prior appearances on The Apprentice, a reality television show formerly hosted by Trump, releases audio recordings of Trump and John Kelly (Trump's White House Chief of Staff) regarding her January 2018 dismissal. Manigault claims that "there are tapes of [Trump] using the N-word repeatedly while filming The Apprentice reality series".

....

August 13, 2018

In a flurry of early-morning tweets, President Trump describes Omarosa Manigault as "wacky", "vicious", "not smart",

"nasty", "a loser", and "a lowlife", and claims that she "begged [Trump] for a job, tears in her eyes".

....

August 13, 2018

President Trump signs legislation named the John S. McCain National Defense Authorization Act while not mentioning the Senator's name.

....

August 14, 2018

President Trump tweets that Omarosa Manigault had been "a crazed, crying lowlife" when he gave her a job at the White House, describing the appointment as Trump giving Manigault "a break"; in the same tweet, Trump called Manigault a "dog". Some commentators express concern that Manigault, whose official title had been Assistant to the President and Director of Communications for Office of Public Liaison, carrying a taxpayer-funded annual salary of $180,000, had been hired out of pity as Trump admits to knowing at the time that she was unqualified for the position.

....

August 15, 2018

President Trump unilaterally revokes the security clearance of former CIA Director John Brennan, citing what Trump alleges to be Brennan's "erratic" behavior, "increasingly frenzied commentary", and his "series of unfounded and outrageous allegations"; many observers agree that this action appears to be retaliation for Brennan's outspokenness on the possible collusion to interfere in the 2016 elections by the Trump campaign and the Russian government

August 15, 2018

President Trump unilaterally revokes the security clearance of former CIA Director John Brennan, citing what Trump alleges to be Brennan's "erratic" behavior, "increasingly frenzied commentary", and his "series of unfounded and outrageous allegations"; In an interview with *The Wall Street Journal*, Trump directly connected the revocation of Brennan's security clearance with his frustration at the ongoing Special Counsel investigation.

August 16, 2018

William McRaven, a navy admiral best known for his role as special operations commander overseeing the raid that killed Osama bin Laden, publicly expresses a political position by authoring an opinion-editorial in The Washington Post in defense of Brennan; McRaven dares Trump to also revoke his security clearance, writing: "I would consider it an honor if you would revoke my security clearance as well, so I can add my name to the list of men and women who have spoken up

against your presidency."

August 16, 2018

Hundreds of newspapers across the United States publish editorials emphasizing the importance of the freedom of the press, a right which is guaranteed by the First Amendment. The newspapers coordinated the publication date of the editorials, but each wrote an editorial independently.

August 17, 2018

President Trump tweets that the military parade scheduled for November 2018 will be postponed due to cost. Trump blames "the local politicians who run Washington, D.C. (poorly)" of price gouging in reporting the estimated cost of the parade as $92 million, which covers $50 million for military equipment and aircraft, and $42 million for municipal costs such as security. Defense Secretary Jim Mattis accuses the individual writing the report asserting the $92 million figure of "probably smoking something that is legal in my state but not in most".

August 19, 2018

In an interview on Meet the Press, a news program on NBC hosted by Chuck Todd, Trump's legal adviser Rudy Giuliani says that "truth isn't truth".

August 20, 2018

President Trump attacks Bruce Ohr, a current senior Justice Department official, asking whether he will "ever be fired". However, there is no evidence that Ohr had any involvement with either the FBI investigation or the Special Counsel investigation.

....

August 20, 2018

The New York Times reports that Trump's former personal attorney, Michael Cohen, is under investigation for bank fraud and tax evasion relating to loans amounting to $20 million, taken for Cohen's taxi medallion venture.

....

August 21, 2018

The first trial of Paul Manafort, former chair of the Trump campaign, concludes, with the jury finding Manafort guilty on five counts of tax evasion, two counts of bank fraud, and one count of failure to disclose a foreign bank account.

....

August 21, 2018

Michael Cohen, Trump's former personal attorney, pleads guilty to five counts of tax evasion, two counts of campaign finance violations, and one count of bank fraud.

....

August 23, 2018

Michael Cohen, Trump's former personal attorney, pleads guilty to five counts of tax evasion, two counts of campaign finance violations, and one count of bank fraud.

fraud.

....

August 23, 2018

David Pecker, the CEO of American Media, Inc. (which owns the National Enquirer magazine), is granted immunity by federal prosecutors in exchange for his testimony.

....

September 3, 2018

President Trump sarcastically tweets "Good job Jeff ..." following the Justice Department indictments of Duncan Hunter and Chris Collins. Trump was criticizing Attorney General Jeff Sessions' handling of the investigations as supporting the Democratic agenda.

....

September 5, 2018

The New York Times publishes an editorial written by an anonymous senior administration official in the Trump administration which is critical of President Trump.The senior Trump administration official assailed President Donald Trump's "amorality" and reckless decision-making and said he or she is part of a "resistance" working to thwart Trump's worst impulses.

....

September 12, 2018

Democrats in the Senate reveal that they have received an allegation of sexual assault against Supreme Court nominee Brett Kavanaugh .Christine Blasey Ford is identified as the source of the sexual assault allegation against Kavanaugh.

....

TRUMP: *Worst. President. Ever.*

2018

September 25, 2018

President Trump addressed the United Nations General Assembly at the Headquarters of the United Nations, and drew laughter from international representatives when he said that the Trump "administration has accomplished more than almost any administration in the history of the United States—"so true". Trump immediately commented that he had not expected that type of reaction.

October 9, 2018

United Nations Ambassador Nikki Haley announces her resignation. However, a source familiar with the situation told CNN that Haley notified Trump about her decision last week and did not tell Secretary of State Mike Pompeo or White House national security adviser John Bolton.

October 11, 2018

President Donald Trump said that he is reluctant to cut off arms sales to Saudi Arabia if the kingdom is found to be responsible for the assumed death of *Washington Post* columnist Jamal Khashoggi, believing such a move could be detrimental to the U.S. economy.

October 17, 2018

Donald McGahn resigns as White House Chief Counsel. He will be replaced by Patrick Cipollone.

October 22, 2018

President Trump attends a political rally at the Toyota Center in Houston, Texas, and claims "I'm a nationalist."

October 24, 2018

President Trump and the White House condemn as "alleged violent attacks" a number of packages containing "potential explosive devices" that were addressed to various Democrats and intercepted by the Secret Service.

October 26, 2018

President Trump opened a rally in Charlotte, North Carolina on Friday decrying "political violence" after pipe bomb suspect Cesar Altieri Sayoc Jr. was charged with sending bombs to 13 prominent Democrats and critics of the president. But that nonpartisan message didn't last long: He then transitioned into a regular Trump rally, complete with the typical "lock her up" chants and attacks on the media.

November 6, 2018

The midterm elections are held with Democrats making significant gains in the House of Representatives and in state elections, while Republicans strengthen their slim hold on the Senate. Gains in the House of Representatives give Democrats

TRUMP: *Worst. President. Ever.*

the majority, and the ability to control committees to investigate President Trump and his administration beginning in January 2019.

November 7, 2018

Attorney General Jeff Sessions resigns at the request of President Trump and is replaced by Matthew Whitaker, Sessions' Chief of Staff.

November 7, 2018

President Trump suspends the access pass of CNN journalist Jim Acosta after he continues to ask questions and refuses to give up the microphone.

November 9, 2018

President Trump berated Prime Minister Teresa May for Great Britain not doing enough in his assessment to contain Iran. He questioned her over Brexit and complained about the trade deals he sees as unfair with European countries.

November 10, 2018

President Trump fails to attend a ceremony at the Aisne Marine American Cemetery in France. He cites poor weather grounding his helicopter, and a desire not to disrupt traffic with his potential motorcade.

November 11, 2018

President Trump fails to attend a ceremony with European leaders in Paris marking the 100th anniversary of the end of World War I.

November 11, 2018

President Trump attends a ceremony at the Arc de Triomphe with 60 other world leaders. French President Emmanuel Macron delivers a speech in which he denounces nationalism as a betrayal of patriotism and warns against 'old demons coming back to wreak chaos and death'. This is seen as a rebuke of President Trump and Russian President Vladimir Putin, who is also in attendance.

November 11, 2018

President Trump returns to Washington where he again misses a ceremony at Arlington National Cemetery marking the 100th anniversary of the end of World War I claiming he was unable to do so because he was "extremely busy on calls for the country".

November 14, 2018

Media reports that President Trump has been in a bad mood since the midterm elections due to the significant Republican losses and is planning to shuffle his staff including Secretary of Homeland Security Kirstjen Nielsen and White House Chief of Staff John Kelly.

November 17, 2018

President Trump visits California to tour the devastation caused by wildfires.[25] He mistakenly refers to the fire ravaged area as "Pleasure" rather than Paradise. Trump also drew criticism for criticising the state's forest management yet again, by suggesting California look to Finland as an example of how to operate."They spent a lot of time on raking and cleaning and doing things and they don't have any problem," Trump remarked.

November 18, 2018

President Trump sits for an interview on *Fox News Sunday* with Chris Wallace. On the Mueller investigation, Trump stated "There was no collusion whatsoever, and the whole thing is a scam." However, to date there have been:
191 criminal counts
35 people/entities charged
6 people pleaded guilty
1 found guilty in trial

November 19, 2018

President Trump criticizes Admiral William McRaven, a Navy Seal and former head of Special Operations Command for not killing Osama bin Laden sooner.

November 20, 2018

President Trump issues a statement called extraordinary and remarkable by the media, declaring unwavering loyalty to Saudi Arabia despite its murder of *Washington Post* columnist Jamal Khashoggi.

November 20, 2018

Details emerge of attempts by President Trump to order the Justice Department to prosecute his political enemies, 2016 presidential election opponent Hillary Clinton and former FBI Director James Comey.

November 20, 2018

President Trump defends Ivanka Trump's use of personal email for official government business declining to acknowledge hypocrisy given his calls for Hillary Clinton to be imprisoned for her use of personal emails during her time as Secretary of State.

November 20, 2018

United States Court of Appeals for the Ninth Circuit, based in San Francisco, rules against President Trump's immigration policy. The President lashes out against the court calling it 'a lawless disgrace' and threatening unspecified retaliation. Chief Justice John G. Roberts issues a rare statement defending the impartiality of courts.

November 20, 2018

After being rebuked by Chief Justie John Roberts, President Trump attacked him,

TRUMP: *Worst. President. Ever.*

tweeting ""Sorry Chief Justice John Roberts, but you do indeed have 'Obama judges,' and they have a much different point of view than the people who are charged with the safety of our country. It would be great if the 9th Circuit was indeed an 'independent judiciary,' but if it is why......".

November 22, 2018

President Trump authorizes troops stationed at the U.S.-Mexican border to use lethal force if deemed necessary and also threatens to close the entire southern border with Mexico. Lethal force by U.S. troops is directly prohibited by Federal law.

November 23, 2020

The day after Thanksgiving 2018, Trump was asked by reporters what he was thankful for that year. To which he responded: "[I'm thankful]...for having made a tremendous difference in this country. I've made a tremendous difference in the country. This country is so much stronger now than it was when I took office that you wouldn't believe it. I mean, you see, but so much stronger people can't even believe it. When I see foreign leaders they say we cannot believe the difference in strength between the United States now and the United States two years ago."

November 23, 2018

The New York Supreme Court rejects a motion by President Trump to have New York State Attorney General's lawsuit against the Trump Foundation dismissed, allowing the case to proceed. The motion was made on the basis of presidential immunity and political bias.

November 25, 2018

U.S. Customs and Border Protection temporarily close all vehicle and pedestrian traffic at the major San Ysidro port of entry between Tijuana, Mexico and San Diego, California and used tear gas on migrants and refugees who approached the border fence.

November 26, 2018

President Trump defends using "safe" tear gas as DHS claims 600 migrants are convicted criminals "First of all, the tear gas is a very minor form of the tear gas itself. It's very safe," he said. "The ones that were suffering to a certain extent were the people that were putting it out there."

November 28, 2018

President Trump uses his Twitter account to retweet an image calling for his political opponents to be imprisoned for treason. The image includes Rod Rosenstein, his own Deputy Attorney General, and Robert Mueller.

2018

November 29, 2018

President Trump's long time lawyer and fixer Michael Cohen pleads guilty to lying to Congress in relation to the Mueller Russia investigation. Trump makes a statement to the media that Cohen was lying to reduce his prison sentence. He further states that there was nothing wrong with his involvement with an ultimately unsuccessful personal business deal with Russia during the 2016 presidential election.

December 1, 2018

President Trump holds a bilateral meeting and dinner with Chinese President Xi Jinping, claiming they have reached an agreement to halt the escalating trade war between the United States and China. The following Tuesday senior officials play down expectations and acknowledged that key provisions were not finalized. Trump tweets that he is a "Tariff Man", causing stock markets to plunge three percent.

December 3, 2018

In a series of tweets, President Trump calls for harsh sentencing of Michael Cohen, following a guilty plea in cooperation with the Mueller investigation. The president also praises longtime associate Roger Stone for not cooperating with Mueller.

December 4, 2018

Senate leaders attend a closed-door security briefing by CIA Director Gina Haspel and emerge from the meeting to effectively accuse President Trump of misleading the country over the killing of Jamal Khashoggi.

December 5, 2018

Lobbyists representing the Saudi government reserved blocks of rooms at President Trump's Washington, D.C., hotel within a month of Trump's election in 2016 — paying for an estimated 500 nights at the luxury hotel in just three months, according to organizers of the trips and documents obtained by *The Washington Post.*

December 6, 2018

President Trump's former Secretary of State Rex Tillerson makes public comments criticizing Trump. Tillerson said Trump is "pretty undisciplined, doesn't like to read" and repeatedly attempted to do illegal things. Trump responds the following day with an attack on Twitter calling Tillerson 'lazy' and 'dumb as a rock'.

December 11, 2018

President Trump meets with Democratic Party congressional leaders Nancy Pelosi and Chuck Schumer in the Oval Office. The meeting is combative, with the president threatening to shut down the government over funding for the Mexican border wall. President Trump declares

TRUMP: *Worst. President. Ever.*

that he would be "proud" to shut down parts of the government if it were to result in a border wall.

December 12, 2018

Michael Cohen, President Trump's former personal lawyer, is sentenced to three years in prison for tax evasion, violation of campaign finance laws and deceiving banks and Congress.

December 13, 2018

Federal prosecutors are examining whether foreigners illegally funneled donations to President Trump's inaugural committee and a pro-Trump super PAC in hopes of buying influence over American policy.

December 15, 2018

Interior Secretary Ryan Zinke tenders his resignation letter, The Justice Department is investigating Zinke for possibly using his office for personal gain following a referral from the Interior Department's inspector general,

December 18, 2018

President Trump agrees to shut down the Donald J. Trump Foundation following an investigation by New York State Attorney General Barbara Underwood which found "a shocking pattern of illegality involving the Trump Foundation -including unlawful coordination with the Trump presidential campaign, repeated and willful self-dealing, and much more".

December 18, 2018

President Trump abandons demands for funding for his border wall, drawing unprecedented criticism from his conservative media allies.

December 19, 2018

President Trump ordered the withdrawal of 2,000 American troops from Syria, bringing a sudden end to a military campaign that largely vanquished the Islamic State but ceding a strategically vital country to Russia and Iran. Aides, officials and allies are blindsided by the decision, which is made without any consultation.

December 19, 2018

A federal judge blocks the Trump Administration attempts to deny asylum to domestic violence victims.

December 20, 2018

Secretary of Defense Jim Mattis announces his resignation, effective February 28, 2019, with a rebuke of President Trump's foreign policy.

December 20, 2018

President Trump ordered the military to begin planning to withdraw about half the troops in Afghanistan. South Carolina GOP Sen. Lindsey Graham said "Based on

TRUMP: *Worst. President. Ever.*

my assessment in Afghanistan, if we withdrew anytime soon, you would be paving the way for a second 9/11,"

December 20, 2018

President Trump reverses again on a federal government shutdown over his border wall, vowing he will not sign any budget extension bill that does not fund the wall. The Senate and House are in stalemate with the former voting for no funding and the latter voting for funding for the wall.

December 20, 2018

North Korea announces that it will not eliminate its nuclear weapons unless the U.S. first removes nuclear weapons and forces from the region. North Korea further accuses President Trump of twisting the agreement made between himself and Kim Jong-un in Singapore on June 22, 2018.

December 21, 2018

CNN reports that President Trump has twice lashed out at acting Attorney General Matthew Whitaker over the prosecution of his former lawyer and fixer Michael Cohen, further reporting that these events underscore the extent to which the President firmly believes the Attorney General of the United States should serve as his personal protector.

December 22, 2018

A government shutdown begins following the failure of Congress and President Trump to reach a compromise on border wall funding.

December 22, 2018

Brett McGurk, special presidential envoy for the Global Coalition to Counter the Islamic State of Iraq and the Levant, resigns effective December 31, 2018, in protest at President Trump's decision to pull American troops from Syria. In response, President Trump wrote that he did not know McGurk and questioned if McGurk was a "grandstander".

December 23, 2018

President Trump, who aides said has been seething about news coverage of Defense Secretary Jim Mattis's pointed resignation letter, abruptly announced Sunday that he was removing Mattis two months before his planned departure and installing Patrick Shanahan as acting defense secretary.

December 23, 2018

While on vacation in Cabo San Lucas, Mexico, Secretary Mnuchin conducts a series of individual calls with the CEO's of America's six largest banks, to affirm adequate liquidity and respond to market volatility.

December 24, 2018

President Trump attacks the Federal

Reserve via Twitter, saying they are the only problem in the economy, which is in a significant downturn. Recent reporting has claimed that the president is seeking to fire the head of the Federal Reserve for raising interest rates.

....

December 24, 2018

In a Christmas Eve call, Trump asked a 7-year-old named Collman Lloyd whether the child still believes in Santa Claus. "Are you still a believer in Santa? Because at 7, it's marginal, right?" Trump asked Collman.

....

December 31, 2018

The first quarter of 2019 began with the continuing government shutdown which had begun on December 22; it lasted until January 25.

....

January 4, 2019

President Trump considers declaring a national emergency on the southern border in order to bypass Congress on the issue of a border wall.

....

January 9, 2019

President Trump abruptly halted spending talks at the White House on Wednesday, after congressional Democrats again rejected his demand for a $5.7 billion border wall.

On Twitter, Trump dismissed the negotiations as a "total waste of time," as a partial government shutdown stretched into its 19th day. He added, "I said

bye-bye, nothing else works!"

....

January 10, 2019

The Trump administration on Thursday defended its decision to lift sanctions on companies linked to the billionaire Russian oligarch Oleg V. Deripaska, despite deep concerns from newly empowered House Democrats that the move was an effort by President Trump to help an ally of President Vladimir V. Putin of Russia.

....

January 12, 2019

The partial government shutdown enters its 22nd day, becoming the longest government shutdown in U.S. history.

....

January 14, 2019

President Trump entertains the Clemson Tigers, 2018 College Football Playoff National Champions, at the White House with a menu of various fast foods.

....

January 15, 2019

The Trump administration said it would require tens of thousands of federal employees back to work without pay to get the government running amid a partial shutdown well into its third week, as the White House and increasingly agitated lawmakers on Capitol Hill cast about for a way to end the stalemate.

....

TRUMP: *Worst. President. Ever.*

January 16, 2019

Speaker Pelosi sends a letter to President Trump that suggests he either reschedule his 2019 State of the Union Address or submit a written State of the Union to Congress instead of a televised oral speech, citing fears of security concerns regarding unpaid Secret Service members as a consequence of the government shutdown.

January 17, 2019

A report by *BuzzFeed News* journalists Jason Leopold and Anthony Cormier is released, alleging that President Trump directed his former attorney Michael Cohen to lie to Congress about their Moscow Tower Project. The report further alleges that Cohen did not reveal this to the Mueller investigation himself, but rather confirmed it when prompted with evidence such as text and e-mail exchanges between implicated parties.

January 23, 2019

President Trump sends a letter to Speaker Pelosi stating that he intends to move forward with the planned date of January 29 for his State of the Union Address.[31] Pelosi blocks his attempt at an address until the government is reopened, making Trump the first President in U.S. history to be uninvited to a State of the Union Address.

January 25, 2019

Roger Stone, a former adviser to President Trump, is indicted by the Mueller investigation and then arrested by the FBI at his Florida home on charges of obstruction, witness tampering and making false statements. He is later released on a $250,000 bond and stripped of his passport.

January 25, 2019

The FAA delays flights at the LaGuardia Airport in New York City, and multiple other major airports, due to safety concerns from staffing shortages as a consequence of the ongoing shutdown.

January 25, 2019

President Trump, from the Rose Garden, says he and Congressional leaders Mitch McConnell and Chuck Schumer have agreed upon a three-week stop-gap spending deal, which does not contain funding for a wall on the southern border, in order to temporarily end the government shutdown. The partial government shutdown ends on its 35th day.

January 28, 2019

The United States Secretary of Homeland Security Kirstjen Nielsen, Acting Attorney General Matthew Whitaker, Commerce Secretary Wilbur Ross, and FBI Director Christopher Wray announce 23 criminal charges against Chinese tech giant Huawei and its CFO Meng Wanzhou.

February 15, 2019

President Trump declares a national emergency in order to secure sufficient funds to construct a physical barrier along the Southern border.

....

March 2, 2019

President Trump gives a speech in Oxon Hill, Maryland to the 2019 Conservative Political Action Conference. Among some gems for the audience:

"How many times did you hear, for months and months, 'There is no way to 270. So I think we're going to do even better in 2020. I think we're going to do numbers that people haven't seen for a long time."

"So they don't have anything with Russia. There's no collusion."

"Number one, I'm in love, and you're in love. We're all in love together."

"And from the day we came down the escalator, I really don't believe we've had an empty seat at any arena, at any stadium."

"By the way, you know I'm building the wall. We're finishing the wall. We got a lot of money. It's in the thing."

"We have people in Congress that hate our country."

....

March 4, 2019

President Trump entertains the North Dakota State Bison, 2018 College Football Playoff National Champions, at the White House with a menu of various fast foods.

....

March 24, 2019

A four-page summary of the Mueller Report was released to Congress and found that President Trump did not collude with the Russians to win the 2016 presidential election and, in the opinion of AG Barr, the issue of whether obstruction of justice was committed was found to be inconclusive.

....

April 4, 2019

President Trump threatens to close the United States–Mexico border within one year if Mexico does not stop the "massive amounts of drugs" coming into the United States.

....

April 5, 2019

President Donald Trump backpedaled on his threat to shut down the southern border, saying Thursday that now he doesn't think the US will "ever have to close the border."

....

April 8, 2019

Secret Service director Randolph Alles to leave his position in May at President Trump's request. Secret Service officials have been caught by surprise with the news and are only finding out through CNN.

....

April 15, 2019

Attorney General William Barr issues an order directing immigration judges to deny posting of bail by asylum seekers.

....

2019

April 16, 2019

President Trump uses the second veto of his Administration on a bipartisan resolution to end American involvement in the military campaign in Yemen. Congress had earlier voted to invoke the War Powers Act of 1973.

May 8, 2019

Refusing to share it's contents, President Trump asserts executive privilege over the full Mueller Report.

May 8, 2019

The House Judiciary Committee, in a 24–16 vote, moves to hold Attorney General William Barr in contempt of Congress for failing to deliver the unredacted version of the Mueller report.

May 8, 2019

House Intelligence Committee issues a subpoena to the Justice Department for all "counterintelligence and foreign intelligence" collected for the pre-redacted version of special counsel Robert Mueller's report.

May 10, 2019

The Trump Administration raises tariffs on $200 billion worth of Chinese imports.

May 10, 2019

House Ways and Means Committee chairman Richard Neal subpoenas the Treasury Department and the Internal Revenue Service for the tax returns of President Trump.

May 20, 2019

A federal judge from the DC District Court denies President Trump's bid to quash a House Oversight Committee subpoena for years of his financial records from his accounting firm. The judge also declined a request by the president's lawyers to stay his order pending their appeal.

May 22, 2019

President Trump leaves a meeting on infrastructure with senior Democrats after only three minutes. Shortly afterwards, he holds a surprise press conference in the Rose Garden.

June 4, 2019

Hope Hicks, a former aide to President Trump, and Annie Donaldson, a former McGahn aide, are instructed by the White House not to comply with House Judiciary Committee subpoenas.

June 14, 2019

The Office of Special Counsel recommends Trump aide Kellyanne Conway be "removed from service" for violating the Hatch Act, which bans federal employees from political activity.

TRUMP: *Worst. President. Ever.*

June 18, 2019

President Trump holds a rally and formally launches his 2020 reelection campaign in Orlando, Florida. During the rally President Trump vowed if "elected to a second term we will cure cancer and ends AIDS' and "come up with the cures to many, many problems, to many, many diseases".

June 19, 2019

EPA administrator Andrew Wheeler announces a roll-back of the Clean Power Plan. States will now be allowed to set their own carbon emissions standards for coal-fired power plants. EPA authority on carbon emissions will be limited going forward.

June 21, 2019

President Trump warns Iran after its Revolutionary Guard acknowledges shooting down an American drone in the Strait of Hormuz. Iran claims the drone "violated Iranian airspace", while U.S. military claims the drone was shot down over "international airspace" and the action was "an unprovoked attack on a U.S. surveillance asset".

June 25, 2019

The Trump administration's chief of protocol in the State Department has been pulled off the job just ahead of the G-20 summit amid an investigation into allegations of discrimination and harassment.

June 26, 2019

EPA official William Wehrum resigns amid claims of possible ethics violations.

June 27, 2019

Supreme Court blocks a citizenship question from being included in the 2020 census and says "the administration provided a contrived justification" for including it.

June 30, 2019

President Trump briefly walks into the northern side of the Joint Security Area of the Korean Demilitarized Zone (DMZ), accompanied by North Korean Leader Kim Jong-Un and becomes the first sitting U.S. President to enter North Korea.

July 12, 2019

Secretary of Labor Alex Acosta resigns amid controversy surrounding the non-prosecution agreement he made with Jeffrey Epstein as the United States attorney for the Southern District of Florida.

July 14, 2019

President Trump tweets that progressive Democratic congresswomen should "go back and help fix the totally broken and crime infested places from which they

TRUMP: *Worst. President. Ever.*

2019

came", drawing widespread criticism, even from some Republicans.

July 17, 2019

The House of Representatives votes to hold Attorney General William Barr and Commerce Secretary Wilbur Ross in contempt over an administration decision to add a citizenship question to the 2020 census.

July 18, 2019

Facing an onslaught of indignation and qualms even from his inner circle, President Donald Trump claimed to be unhappy his rally crowd broke into chants of "send her back" as he denigrated a Democratic lawmaker he'd previously said should leave the US.

July 25, 2019

During a phone conversation with the newly elected Ukrainian president Volodymr Zelensky, President Trump repeatedly presses him to open an investigation into Hunter Biden, the son of potential 2020 presidential candidate and former vice president Joe Biden.

July 26, 2019

The Supreme Court rules in a 5–4

decision that President Trump may use military funding for construction of the border wall.

July 27, 2019

President Trump draws criticism for his tweet describing Congressman Elijah Cummings' Baltimore, Maryland, district as a "disgusting, rat and rodent infested mess".

August 2, 2019

President Trump announced that Rep. John Ratcliffe, his embattled pick to lead the nation's intelligence community, was withdrawing from consideration and will remain in Congress after lawmakers raised questions about his qualifications and whether he had padded his résumé.

August 3, 2019

Twenty-three people are killed and 24 injured at a Walmart Supercenter in El Paso, Texas. The suspect, Patrick Crusius, is captured by police.

August 4, 2019

A mass shooting occurs in the Oregon District of Dayton, Ohio, at 1:00 a.m.—less than 24 hours after the El Paso shootings—leaving nine dead and at least 27 injured. The gunman, Connor Stephen Betts, is killed at the scene attempting to enter the Ned Peppers Bar.

August 4, 2019

TRUMP: *Worst. President. Ever.*

In New Jersey, President Trump declares "hate has no place in our country" and suggests that mental illness played a role in both shootings.

....

August 16, 2019

President Trump expresses interest in purchasing Greenland from Denmark. Both Danish and Greenlandic officials reject the proposal.

....

August 20, 2019

President Trump asserts that any Jew who votes for a Democrat is either, "disloyal or unintelligent".

....

August 21, 2019

President Trump proclaims "I am the chosen one" to reporters at the White House.

....

August 22, 2019

President Trump presents the Presidential Medal of Freedom to NBA legend Bob Cousy. He also jokingly adds he would like to "give myself a Medal of Honor".

....

August 23, 2019

President Trump asserts that he reserves the"absolute" right to order U.S. companies to stop doing business with China.

....

August 24, 2019

President Trump walked into a 'nightmare' G7 of a summit of world leaders in an increasingly isolated position, facing an increasingly troubled global economic environment.

....

August 26, 2019

President Trump fails to attend the G7 discussion on climate, biodiversity, and the Amazon forest fires. The White House makes false claims stating Trump was attending other engagements with German chancellor Angela Merkel and Indian prime minister Narendra Modi. Both leaders attend the climate session.

....

August 28, 2019

President Trump announces a new administration rule that citizenship will no longer be automatic for children of some U.S. military members living overseas.

....

August 29, 2019

The Trump administration and the Environmental Protection Agency (EPA) announce a reduction of restrictions on the production of Methane, a powerful greenhouse gas.

....

August 30, 2019

President Trump tweets a high-resolution aerial image of a failed Iranian missile launch. Satellite tracking analysts concluded the image was likely taken by the USA-224 reconnaissance

TRUMP: *Worst. President. Ever.* 63

satellite. Some intelligence veterans expressed dismay that Trump tweeted the image from a classified briefing.

August 31, 2019

A mass shooting occurs in the cities of Midland and Odessa, Texas, leaving seven dead and 22 injured. The perpetrator, Seth Ator, is shot by police and dies at the scene.

September 1, 2019

Trump tweeted that Alabama was one of the states at greater risk from Hurricane Dorian than had been initially forecast. The federal weather office in Birmingham then tweeted that, actually, Alabama would be unaffected by the storm.

September 10, 2019

National Security Advisor John Bolton resigns following President Trump's request the day before.

September 13, 2019

Trump administration opens huge reserve in Alaska to drilling.

September 18, 2019

President Trump announces on Twitter

that he is revoking California's ability to set its own auto emissions standards.

September 24, 2019

While at the United Nations, President Trump tweets that he will release a memorandum of his July phone call to Ukrainian President Volodymyr Zelensky, in which they reportedly discussed Joe Biden, Hunter Biden, and the 2020 American election.

September 24, 2019

Speaker of the House Nancy Pelosi announces that the House of Representatives will launch a formal impeachment inquiry against President Trump.

September 25, 2019

A whistleblower complaint that was filed on August 12 is declassified and released to the public by a 421–0 vote in the House of Representatives. It accuses President Trump of "abus[ing] his office for personal gain" by "[soliciting] interference" from Ukraine in the 2020 election and that the White House took steps to cover it up"

September 26, 2019

Addressing the U.S. Mission to the United Nations, Trump states of the news media:'You know, these animals in the press. They're animals. Some of the worst human beings you'll ever meet... They're scum, many of them are scum.'

TRUMP: *Worst. President. Ever.*

September 26, 2019

The Administration says it plans to allow only 18,000 refugees to resettle in the United States in the 2020 fiscal year, its lowest level since the modern program began in 1980.

....

September 27, 2019

President Trump's special envoy for Ukraine Kurt Volker resigns amid reports that he introduced Trump's personal attorney, Rudy Giuliani, to Ukrainian officials.

....

September 30, 2019

A White House official reports that President Trump pressured Australian prime minister Scott Morrison to find information for a Justice department inspection of the Mueller investigation in an attempt to destroy said investigation.

....

October 1, 2019

President Trump accuses the impeachment inquiry against him of being a coup d'état, designed to strip Americans of their freedoms.

....

October 2, 2019

President Trump holds a bilateral meeting and joint press conference with Finnish president Sauli Niinistö at the White House. While responding to reporters about the impeachment inquiry, President Trump calls Adam Schiff a "low life" and the whistle-blower's source a "spy".

....

October 2, 2019

President Trump expresses interest in building an electrified moat filled with alligators along the southern border with Mexico, forcing his aides to find a cost estimate. He also proposes shooting migrants in the legs in order to slow them down and threatens to close the 2,000 mile border with Mexico in an effort to control immigration.

....

October 3, 2019

President Trump publicly urges China and Ukrainian president Volodymyr Zelensky to investigate former Vice President Joe Biden and his family on national television.

....

October 7, 2019

The Trump administration announces it is adding 28 Chinese corporations to a blacklist over concerns of the role the companies played in human rights violations, barring American companies from doing business with these companies.

....

October 8, 2019

The Trump administration announces in a letter to Speaker of the House Nancy Pelosi that it will not cooperate in any way with the impeachment inquiry, calling it "illegitimate" and "dangerous", effectively challenging Congress's constitutional power.

October 11, 2019

Acting Secretary of Homeland Security Kevin McAleenan, the fourth person to serve in that post during the Trump presidency, resigns.

October 11, 2019

Secretary of State Mike Pompeo defends President Trump's call with the Ukrainian president and accuses Democratic members of Congress of "trying to take down this president", saying that is commonplace to ask allies to "do things for us".

October 11, 2019

Former U.S. Ambassador to Ukraine Marie Yovanovitch, in defiance of a White House ban on cooperating with Congress, tells the House impeachment inquiry that Trump personally pressured the State Department to have her ousted from her position.

October 14, 2019

President Trump falsely claims that Kurdish soldiers—former allies in the War against ISIS—are releasing ISIS POWs during the Turkish invasion of Syria following President Trump's order for U.S. troops to vacate the country.

October 14, 2019

President Trump announces sanctions on Turkey following backlash from Republican Party congressmen over the president's withdrawal of American troops stationed in Syria.

October 16, 2019

The House of Representatives formally condemns President Trump's withdrawal of troops from Syria by a vote of 354–60.

October 16, 2019

President Trump holds a White House meeting with key Democrats and Republicans on Syria. After the meeting, House Speaker Nancy Pelosi and some Democrats contend that the president was "having a meltdown", calling the speaker a "third-rate politician".

October 17, 2019

Acting White House chief of staff Mick Mulvaney confirms Trump blocked military aid to Ukraine in order to force investigation of his political rivals. Mulvaney called the quid pro quo exchange "absolutely appropriate" and "we do that all the time with foreign policy."

October 17, 2019

Acting White House chief of staff Mick Mulvaney defends President Trump's decision to hold the 2020 G-7 summit at the Trump National Doral Miami Golf Club.

....

October 19, 2019

In response to fierce criticism from Congress, President Trump announces on Twitter that he will no longer be holding the 2020 G-7 summit at Trump National Doral Miami, instead considering Camp David as a possible alternative.

....

October 19, 2019

Energy Secretary Rick Perry said on Thursday that he plans to leave his post later this year after he informed President Donald Trump of his intention to resign. Perry's resignation comes amid scrutiny over his role in the Trump administration's dealings with Ukraine. White House acting chief of staff Mick Mulvaney confirmed Thursday that the President asked Perry to work with Trump's personal lawyer, Rudy Giuliani, on policies related to Ukraine.

....

October 21, 2019

During an interview on Fox News with Sean Hannity, Donald Trump says both The New York Times and The Washington Post treat him terribly with very negative stories and that he will cancel White House subscriptions to these newspapers.

....

October 24, 2019

A federal judge holds that Education Secretary Betsy DeVos is in contempt of court for violating an order to stop collecting on student loans.

....

October 27, 2019

President Trump confirms that ISIS leader Abu Bakr al-Baghdadi detonated an explosive vest in a confrontation with American troops in northwest Syria, killing himself and three of his six children.

....

October 29, 2019

Director of the National Security Council (NSA) Lieutenant Colonel Alexander S. Vindman testifies to the House Impeachment inquiry about outside influencers who promoted "a false and alternative narrative" that was not helpful "to U.S. national security".

....

November 3, 2019

President Trump blames Governor Gavin Newsom for the many wildfires that are currently raging across California and threatens to withhold funding to fight the fires on Twitter. Trump tweets that Newsom has "done a terrible job of forest management", causing the string of recent fires. Of the 33 million acres of forest in California, 57% is

TRUMP: *Worst. President. Ever.*

controlled by the federal government.

November 7, 2019

A New York State Judge orders President Trump to pay two million dollars to various non-profit organizations for his abuse of the Trump Foundation to advance his 2016 presidential campaign.

November 14, 2019

A mass shooting occurs at Saugus High School in Santa Clarita, California, killing two and injuring three others. The suspect, 16 year-old Nathaniel Berhow is critically injured and dies the next day.

November 16, 2019

President Trump makes an unscheduled visit to Walter Reed National Military Medical Center to "begin portions of his routine annual physical exam" that included a "quick exam and labs", according to the White House. There is no precedent for unscheduled hospital visits outside of medical emergencies.

November 24, 2019

Secretary of the Navy Richard V. Spencer is fired by Secretary of Defense Mark Esper over a dispute between President Trump and Spencer after the president intervened in the war crimes trial of Chief Petty Officer Eddie Gallagher, a Navy SEAL commando.

November 25, 2019

A federal judge rules that former White House counsel Don McGahn must be allowed to testify to the House impeachment inquiry, overruling President Trump's assertion of executive privilege over McGahn, adding that "presidents are not kings."

December 4, 2019

The House impeachment inquiry invites four legal scholars to testify whether President Trump's actions concerning Ukraine warranted impeachment. Three scholars said the president's actions did require impeachment, saying that Trump's conduct was worse than any preceding president.

December 11, 2019

President Trump signs an executive order defining Judaism as a nationality or race, not just as a religion, in response to increased anti-Semitism in universities.

December 18, 2019

President Trump is impeached by the House of Representatives on charges of abuse of power and obstruction of Congress in a vote of 230–197 on the first article and 229–198 on the second article of impeachment.

December 19, 2019

Christianity Today, a conservative evangelical

TRUMP: *Worst. President. Ever.*

Christian magazine, publishes an editorial calling for President Trump to be "removed from office" due to his violation of the Constitution and "profoundly immoral actions".

....

December 21, 2019

President Trump complains that windmills are "very expensive", claiming that they "kill many bald eagles" and that "he has studied [wind power] better than anybody" during a speech to a group of young conservative supporters in West Palm Beach, Florida.

....

December 27, 2019

The Federal Reserve releases a study showing that President Trump's tariffs have led to both job losses and higher consumer prices.

....

December 29, 2019

The U.S. Department of Defense reports a series of airstrikes against Kata'ib Hezbollah's weapons depots and command centers in Iraq and Syria, reportedly killing at least 25 militiamen and wounding 55 more.

....

December 31, 2019

The American embassy in Iraq is attacked by protestors angered by U.S. air strikes targeting the Iran-backed militia group,

Kataib Hezbollah.

....

January 2, 2020

Major General Qasem Soleimani, Iran's top security and intelligence commander, is killed in an airstrike at Baghdad International Airport. The Department of Defense issues a statement that the strike had been carried out "at the direction of the President". Trump added "Soleimani was plotting imminent and sinister attacks on American diplomats and military personnel, but we caught him in the act and terminated him".

....

January 3, 2020

President Trump threatens on Twitter to attack Iranian cultural sites if Iran retaliates for the assassination of General Soleimani.

....

January 7, 2020

The Pentagon verifies an attack on U.S. forces: "At approximately 5:30 p.m. (EST) on January 7, Iran launched more than a dozen ballistic missiles against U.S. military and coalition forces in Iraq."

....

January 8, 2020

Ukrainian Airlines Flight 752 crashes on departure from Tehran International Airport, killing all 176 passengers aboard. It was mistakenly targeted by Iran as a U.S. cruise missile and shot down.

....

2020

January 9, 2020

The House votes to limit the president's ability to order military operations against Iran, unless explicitly authorized by Congress.

January 10, 2020

In an interview with Fox News's Laura Ingraham, President Trump says Iran had been targeting four American embassies before he ordered the killing of Soleimani. "I can reveal that I believe it would've been four embassies."

January 16, 2020

The United States–Mexico–Canada Agreement (USMCA), President Trump's replacement for the North American Free Trade Agreement (NAFTA), is ratified by the Senate 89–10.

January 22, 2020

President Trump is asked about the coronavirus: "We have it totally under control. It's one person coming in from China. It's going to be just fine."

January 31, 2020

President Trump signs an executive order adding six more countries to his ban on travel from certain mainly-Muslim countries. The added countries are Nigeria, Myanmar, Eritrea, Kyrgyzstan, Sudan, and Tanzania.

February 2, 2020

The Trump administration announces travel restrictions on air traffic to and from China take effect. Secretary of Health and Human Services Alex Azar declares that COVID-19 "poses a public health emergency in the United States".

February 4, 2020

Senator Susan Collins (R-ME) announces that she will vote to acquit President Trump in his impeachment trial, despite saying that what he did was wrong. Collins says her decision is based on the fact that she believes Trump has learned from this case" and "will be more careful in the future".

February 5, 2020

President Trump is acquitted by the United States Senate on charges of abuse of power and obstruction of Congress, 48–52 on the first article and 47–53 on the second. Senator Mitt Romney (R-UT) votes to convict in President Trump's impeachment trial on Article I, becoming the only Republican to do so and the first senator from the same party as the president to vote for removal from office.

February 7, 2020

President Trump fires Lieutenant Colonel Alexander Vindman and ambassador Gordon Sondland in retaliation for their cooperation in his impeachment inquiry.

TRUMP: *Worst. President. Ever.*

Vindman's brother is also fired and escorted from the White House.

February 11, 2020

The Justice Department announces that it will overrule federal prosecutors in the trial of Trump associate Roger Stone and seek a shorter sentence than what the prosecutors had recommended. This comes after President Trump had complained on Twitter that the sentence the prosecutors had been recommending to Stone was "unfair" and a "miscarriage of justice".

February 11, 2020

In response to the DoJ request for a reduced sentence, all four prosecutors (Michael Marando, Adam Jed, Jonathan Kravis and Aaron Zelinsky) withdraw from the Stone trial.

February 12, 2020

Jessie Liu, the U.S. attorney who headed the prosecutions of Roger Stone and Michael Flynn, resigns after President Trump's withdrawal of her nomination as the Treasury Department's undersecretary for terrorism and financial crimes.

February 13, 2020

President Trump publicly acknowledges sending Rudy Giuliani to Ukraine in an attempt to find damaging information on Joe and Hunter Biden, despite his fervent denials of such a search during his impeachment inquiry and trial.

February 14, 2020

Army Secretary Ryan McCarthy announces that the Army will not investigate or take any disciplinary action against Lieutenant Colonel Alexander Vindman in spite of President Trump's comment that the military should "take a look at" whether Vindman said "horrible things" about him.

February 16, 2020

More than 2,000 former Justice Department officials present an open letter strongly condemning President Trump and Attorney General William Barr's "interference in the fair administration of justice", and call on Barr to resign due to his involvement in the Stone case.

February 18, 2020

President Trump commutes the sentences of eleven individuals, including former Illinois governor Rod Blagojevich, who was convicted of attempting to sell a seat in the U.S. Senate, former NYPD commissioner Bernie Kerik, financier Mike Milken, and Eddie DeBartolo Jr., all of whom were convicted on corruption charges.

TRUMP: *Worst. President. Ever.*

February 20, 2020

President Trump fires acting director of national intelligence, Joseph Maguire, after last weeks briefing to the House Intelligence Committee by the top election security official, Shelby Pierson, on Russian interference in the upcoming 2020 election. The president announced that he was replacing Maguire with loyalist Richard Grenell, the current ambassador to Germany, who will oversee 17 U.S. intelligence agencies.

February 20, 2020

Roger Stone is sentenced to 40 months in prison for, in the words of Judge Amy Berman Jackson, "covering up for the president".

February 25, 2020

Supreme Court Justices Sonia Sotomayor and Ruth Bader Ginsburg are attacked on Twitter by President Trump as he demands that they recuse themselves from "all Trump, or Trump-related" cases.

February 25, 2020

In a press briefing at the White House, Nancy Messonnier, Director of National Center for Immunization and Respiratory Diseases warned of the impending community spread of the coronavirus in the United States, stating: "Disruption to everyday life might be severe."

February 26, 2020

At the onset of the COVID-19 pandemic, President Trump announces vice-president Mike Pence to be in charge of the U.S. coronavirus response. This is widely seen to be an attempt to distance Trump politically from any fallout from the potential epidemic.

February 26, 2020

President Trump accused his Democratic critics of "politicizing" the coronavirus virus as he rallied supporters in North Charleston a day before the Democratic primary in South Carolina. Trump dismissed the complaints from Democrats about his handling of the virus as "their new hoax" and insisted "we are totally prepared."

February 28, 2020

President Trump tweets that he will nominate Representative John Ratcliffe (R-TX) to be his director of national intelligence, the second time the President has attempted to make the loyalist lawmaker his spy chief. Ratcliffe had been nominated as Trump's DNI pick after Dan Coats stepped down from the post in July 2019, but the Texas congressman withdrew his name from consideration after lawmakers from both parties raised concerns about his qualifications.

February 29, 2020

TRUMP: *Worst. President. Ever.*

The first patient death in the United States from COVID-19 is reported by Washington state health officials, as state health officials declare a state of emergency.

March 2, 2020

President Trump meets with representatives from numerous pharmaceutical companies in an effort to develop an efficient plan to develop a vaccine and treatments for COVID-19.

March 3, 2020

President Trump speaks to the press concerning the COVID-19 pandemic in the United States after Trump was criticized for his delayed response to the virus. Trump also disputed the World Health Organization's (WHO) official mortality rate for the virus of 3.4%, instead claiming the death rate to be "a fraction of 1%".

March 6, 2020

While visiting the CDC center in Atlanta, Georgia, President Trump praises the CDC's response to the coronavirus. Trump also calls Washington state governor Jay Inslee "a snake" for criticizing his response to the COVID-19 pandemic after Inslee called on Trump to "[stick] to the science and [tell] the truth".

March 6, 2020

President Trump fires acting Chief of Staff Mick Mulvaney and announces Representative Mark Meadows (R-NC) as his replacement.

March 11, 2020

President Trump addresses the nation on prime-time television concerning the COVID-19 pandemic as the total number of confirmed cases passes a thousand. During the address, Trump announces that he will suspend all travel to and from Europe for thirty days, starting midnight Friday. The United Kingdom is exempt from this restriction.

March 12, 2020

Due to the COVID-19 pandemic, the Dow Jones Industrial Average (DJIA) drops ten percent—its worst day since 1987.

March 13, 2020

President Trump declares a national emergency to mitigate the COVID-19 pandemic. The declaration opens access to $50 billion in emergency funding, lifts restrictions on doctors and hospitals, and waives student loan interest.[129] When challenged about the slow response to provide testing, Trump blamed prior administrations saying, "I don't take responsibility at all."

March 16, 2020

In a press conference at the White House, President Trump urges Americans to avoid gatherings of more than ten people, warning

TRUMP: *Worst. President. Ever.*

that the COVID-19 pandemic could last into the summer.

March 16, 2020

The Dow Jones Industrial Average (DJIA) falls 2,997 points, losing 12.9% in its largest point drop ever.

March 18, 2020

President Trump signs the Families First Coronavirus Response Act, a bill providing sick leave, unemployment benefits, free coronavirus testing, and food and medical aid to people affected by the COVID-19 pandemic, into law.

March 18, 2020

In an effort to mitigate the COVID-19 pandemic, President Trump and Canadian prime minister Justin Trudeau close the border between the United States and Canada, allowing only essential traffic through.

March 21, 2020

President Trump announces in a press conference that he will invoke the Defense Production Act to increase production of hospital masks, saying he views the country as entering a wartime setting and that he is "a wartime president".

March 24, 2020

In a virtual town hall held at the White House, President Trump declares that his hope is that the American economy will open back up by Easter Sunday, eliciting concerns from the medical and scientific community. He also expressed desire to ease social distancing restrictions set up to control the spread of coronavirus.

March 25, 2020

The Senate passes the $2 trillion Coronavirus Aid, Relief, and Economic Security Act (H.R. 748), also known as the CARES Act, in a vote of 96–0.

March 27, 2020

In a press conference on the COVID-19 pandemic, President Trump announces that the government will buy more than 100,000 ventilators to meet growing demand. Officials are doubtful whether they can be produced in time to help hospitals that are currently overwhelmed with patients.

April 1, 2020

President Trump reveals that his decision to extend the social distancing guidelines to April 30 was motivated by models which predicted that if the restrictions were removed as many as 2.2 million people would die and about half the country would be infected.[2] President Trump also warned that between 100,000 and 240,000 Americans could become infected in the coming days, despite strict isolation and distancing guidelines.

....

April 2, 2020

Acting Secretary of the Navy Thomas Modly announces he has relieved Captain Brett Crozier from the USS Theodore Roosevelt (CVN-71) for going outside the chain of command for help with 114 positive coronavirus cases on board the aircraft carrier.

....

April 2, 2020

In the daily coronavirus press conference, Jared Kushner declares that the "notion of the federal stockpile was it's supposed to be our stockpile; it's not supposed to be state stockpiles that they then use."

....

April 3, 2020

President Trump notifies Congress he has "removed from office" Intelligence Community Inspector General Michael Atkinson, the individual who had informed Congress about the whistleblower complaint that led to the Ukraine probe and the president's impeachment.

....

April 7, 2020

President Trump announces that Kayleigh McEnany will become the 31st White House press secretary, replacing Stephanie Grisham, who was moved to be the First Lady's chief of staff.

....

April 7, 2020

President Trump dismisses Glenn A. Fine as acting inspector general for the Defense Department, making him ineligible to chair the recently created Pandemic Response Accountability Committee that he had been appointed to eight days previously.

....

April 7, 2020

Acting Navy Secretary Thomas Modly submits a letter of resignation to Defense Secretary Mark Esper, after calling aircraft carrier Captain Crozier "stupid".

....

April 15, 2020

President Trump announces that the US will stop funding the World Health Organization (WHO), after Trump criticized the WHO for being too lenient on China.

....

April 15, 2020

President Trump on Wednesday threatened to use his executive power to force both chambers of Congress to adjourn if the Senate did not confirm his nominees for vacancies across the administration. The National Constitution Center noted that "no President has ever exercised" the authority.

....

April 16, 2020

President Trump announces that the

TRUMP: *Worst. President. Ever.*

states can begin lifting restrictions for coronavirus by May 1 while acknowledging that the decision to reopen is best left to the states.

....

April 17, 2020

President Trump openly encourages far-right political groups to protest social distancing restrictions and calls on states to lift restrictions.

....

April 20, 2020

President Trump announces on Twitter that he will temporarily suspend all immigration in an effort to protect America from "the Invisible Enemy".

....

April 22, 2020

Health Dept. official Dr. Rick Bright is fired by President Trump after questioning the effectiveness of Hydroxychloroquine as a drug to treat COVID-19 and requesting extensive tests to confirm Trump's claims.

....

April 24, 2020

At the daily coronavirus press briefing, President Trump promotes the use of ultraviolet light as a remedy to COVID-19, and muses about injecting bleach or disinfectant into the lungs or other areas of the body to kill the virus.

....

April 29, 2020

Despite the number of novel coronavirus cases surpassing one million in the U.S., President Donald Trump on Wednesday continued to push to reopen the country, with new numbers out that show the country's economy shrank nearly 5% in the first three months of this year, the biggest quarterly decline since the Great Recession.

"This is going away," Trump said, rejecting the idea of a 'new normal' in America. "I want to go back to where it was."

....

May 1, 2020

President Trump dismisses Acting Health and Human Services inspector general Christi Grimm, who had issued an April report describing severe shortages of coronavirus testing materials and personal protective equipment.

....

May 3, 2020

During a Fox News town hall in the Lincoln Memorial, President Trump revises his forecast for the death toll from COVID-19, increasing it to 100,000. He also admits the disease has been more lethal than he expected, adding that early intelligence briefings indicated the virus was "not a big deal".

....

May 7, 2020

One of Trump's personal valets tests positive for coronavirus. White House staffers, including valets, generally do not wear masks. Trump claims, however, that

TRUMP: *Worst. President. Ever.*

he requires all his aides to take rapid tests for the virus before he travels anywhere with them.

....

May 7, 2020

The Justice Department announces that it is dropping all charges against President Trump's former National Security Advisor, Michael Flynn. Flynn had already plead guilty to several crimes.

....

May 8, 2020

Katie Miller, the top spokesperson for Vice President Mike Pence, tests positive for coronavirus. She is married to Stephen Miller, a top aide and speechwriter for President Trump. This suggests multiple people who work in the West Wing may have been exposed.

....

May 10, 2020

Despite the coronavirus diagnosis for one of his staff members, Vice President Pence said he would not self-isolate and would continue to work in person at the White House. Other members of the coronavirus Task Force, including Drs. Redfield, Hahn, and Fauci, however, planned to self-isolate.

....

May 11, 2020

During a press conference, CBS News White House correspondent Weijia Jiang asks President Trump, "Why is this a global competition to you if every day Americans are still losing their lives?" referring to the number of coronavirus

tests performed daily. Trump responds by saying, "They're losing their lives everywhere in the world. And maybe that's a question you should ask China. Don't ask me, ask China that question, OK?".

....

May 16, 2020

President Trump fires Inspector General of the Department of State Steve Linick, following reports that Linick was investigating Secretary of State Mike Pompeo over reports of abuse of office.

....

May 18, 2020

President Trump reveals that he is taking Hydroxychloroquine, an anti-malarial drug untested for its effectiveness against COVID-19, despite FDA warnings that it may cause serious heart problems.

....

May 26, 2020

Glenn Fine, the Defense Department Principal Deputy Inspector General, submitted his resignation, effective June 1. Fine provided leadership of the coronavirus accountability review of emergency funds.

....

May 27, 2020

President Trump threatens to close or

TRUMP: *Worst. President. Ever.*

impose regulation on social media after Twitter flags his post on mail-in ballots as inaccurate.

....

May 28, 2020

President Trump signs an executive order limiting the legal protection that social media companies have, allowing federal agencies and regulators to hold them liable if found to be violating free speech protections by deleting posts or user accounts.

....

May 29, 2020

President Trump warns on Twitter that the "THUGS" using the protests of the murder of George Floyd, to loot and destroy businesses in Minneapolis would be shot if looting continued, adding that "when the looting starts, the shooting starts."

....

May 31, 2020

In an early morning tweet President Trump declares the United States of America will be designating ANTIFA as a terrorist organization. Antifa is a left-wing anti-fascist and anti-racist political movement in the United States.

....

May 31, 2020

News reports surface claiming that on

Friday night Secret Service agents rushed President Trump to a White House bunker as hundreds of protesters gathered outside the executive mansion, some of them throwing rocks and tugging at police barricades.

....

June 1, 2020

In a conference call with the nation's governors, President Trump declares that Chairman of the Joint Chiefs of Staff Mark A. Milley, the nation's highest-ranking military officer, was "in charge" of the response to protests. The nature of Milley's position was not specified, nor the legal authority under which he would assume such a position.

....

June 1, 2020

President Trump delivers a speech in the Rose Garden declaring that he was "dispatching thousands and thousands of heavily armed soldiers, military personnel and law enforcement officers to stop the rioting, looting, vandalism, assaults and the wanton destruction of property," and, "If a city or state refuses to take the actions that are necessary ... then I'll deploy the United States military and quickly solve the problem for them."

....

June 1, 2020

After the press conference at the Rose Garden, Trump walks to the nearby St. John's Church, where an adjacent building had experienced a fire the previous night, in Lafayette Square for a photo op. In preparation for Trump's arrival, riot police and military police use tear gas and stun grenades to clear peaceful protesters assembled at the park. and the clergy at the church.

June 2, 2020

President Trump triggered sharp condemnation from top religious leaders for the second time in two days on Tuesday, with Washington Archbishop Wilton Gregory slamming his visit to a D.C. shrine honoring Pope John Paul II. "I find it baffling and reprehensible that any Catholic facility would allow itself to be so egregiously misused and manipulated in a fashion that violates our religious principles, which call us to defend the rights of all people, even those with whom we might disagree," Gregory said in a statement as Trump and first lady Melania Trump arrived at the Saint John Paul II National Shrine in Northeast Washington.

June 3, 2020

President Trump announces that the Republican National Committee would move the 2020 Republican National Convention from Charlotte, NC to another location, after North Carolina Governor Roy Cooper did not find the health and safety measures put forth by the Republican National Committee to be adequate.

June 9, 2020

President Trump asserts on Twitter that Martin Gugino, elderly man pushed to the ground by police in Buffalo, New York, during a protest over the killing of George Floyd could be a "set up" that Gugino was an "ANTIFA provocateur".

June 15, 2020

The Supreme Court rules in a 5-4 decision that LGBT rights are protected against discrimination by the Civil Rights Act of 1964.

June 16, 2020

The Trump administration announces that it is ordering former National Security Advisor John Bolton to cease publication of his new book, claiming that it violates non-disclosure agreements and releases classified information.

June 18, 2020

The Supreme Court rules in a 5-4 decision that President Trump may not immediately end Deferred Action for Childhood Arrivals (DACA), saying that the Administration did not provide "a reasoned explanation for its action".

June 18, 2020

Mary Elizabeth Taylor, the first black woman to serve as assistant Secretary of State for Legislative Affairs, resigns, stating President Trump's "comments and actions surrounding racial injustice...cut sharply against my core values and conviction".

TRUMP: *Worst. President. Ever.*

June 19, 2020

Geoffrey Berman, the top US attorney in the Sothern District of New York, declines to leave his post after Attorney General William Barr announces his removal and replacement earlier in the evening.

June 20, 2020

President Trump removes Geoffrey Berman as head attorney for the SDNY after he refuses to step down the previous evening.

June 20, 2020

President Trump holds a rally in Tulsa, Oklahoma. Two Secret Service agents at the event test positive for coronavirus; the Secret Service later asks all agents who worked at the event to self-quarantine at home for 14 days.

June 25, 2020

The Trump administration files a brief asking the Supreme Court to invalidate the Affordable Care Act.

June 26, 2020

The New York Times breaks a story about bounties being paid by Russia to Taliban militants to kill American and coalition forces currently stationed in Afghanistan.

June 29, 2020

Director of National Intelligence John Ratcliffe, White House chief of staff Mark Meadows, and national security adviser Robert C. O'Brien conduct a briefing for GOP lawmakers at the White House concerning intelligence suggesting Russia financed Taliban militants to target US and coalition troops.

July 7, 2020

President Trump informs Congress and the United Nations that the United States will formally withdraw from the World Health Organization (WHO), effective July 6, 2021.

July 9, 2020

The Supreme Court rules 7-2 that House Democrats may not access President Trump's tax returns, but also determined that he is not immune to a subpoena for his returns from a New York prosecutor.

July 10, 2020

The Supreme Court rules 7-2 that House Democrats may not access President Trump's tax returns, but also determined that he is not immune to a subpoena for his returns from a New York prosecutor.

July 14, 2020

The Trump administration orders hospitals to forego sending all coronavirus patient information to the CDC and instead submit it to a central database maintained by the Department of Health and Human Services.

effective on August 7.

July 21, 2020

President Trump announces plans to deploy federal law enforcement officers to "Democrat" cities to quell ongoing protests over racism and police brutality. Chicago Mayor Lori Lightfoot expressed concern saying, "We don't need federal agents without any insignia taking people off the streets and holding them, I think, unlawfully."

July 22, 2020

Calling the protests in Portland, Oregon "worse than Afghanistan," President Trump defended the use of excessive force against the peaceful protestors by officers in military camouflage fatigues.

July 28, 2020

Without any evidence that mail-in ballots increase electoral fraud, President Trump continues to suggest that the November election should be delayed.

July 30, 2020

The U.S. GDP indicator declined 9.5% during the second quarter of 2020, the most drastic decline in 70 years.

August 5, 2020

Stephen Akard, the acting State Department's inspector general, resigns after less than three months. His deputy, Diana Shaw is appointed as the temporary acting inspector general

August 6, 2020

President Trump signs executive orders banning the use of TikTok and WeChat in the United States within 45 days if their Chinese parent companies refuse to sell them as a result of national security concerns.

August 9, 2020

President Trump speaks with South Dakota Gov. Kristi Noem about the possibility of adding his own visage to Mount Rushmore. Gov. Noem had a Mount Rushmore replica made with Trump's face on it and presented it to him.

August 25, 2020

President Trump and Postmaster General Louis DeJoy are sued by the states of New York and New Jersey over changes to postal service operations such as the removal of mailboxes and mail sorting machines, the curtailing of overtime hours and the implementation of additional service reductions.

August 27, 2020

President Trump delivers acceptance speech at the Republican National Convention at the South Lawn of the White House. Saying he "profoundly" accepted the nomination for a second term he spoke for 70-minutes on the South Lawn of the White House. He repeatedly misrepresented his record while leveling false or misleading attacks on Democrats, blaming them for America's problems.

September 1, 2020

While discussing the shooting of Jacob Blake, President Trump compares police officers to golfers who might "choke" while attempting a putt.

September 2, 2020

President Trump urges North Carolina voters to cast two votes in the upcoming presidential election, once by mail and then again in person, in order to test his unsubstantiated claims that mail-in voting is prone to fraud.

September 4, 2020

A memo to government agencies from the Office of Management and Budget calls on all agencies to ceases funding for diversity training. labelling it "divisive and anti-American propaganda".

September 4, 2020

President Trump disputes reports in the Atlantic magazine that he has called dead American service members "losers" and those signing to serve in the armed service as "suckers".

September 8, 2020

The Department of Justice takes over the defense of the President in a defamation lawsuit accusing him of sexual assault.

September 10, 2020

President Trump holds a news conference and debates with journalists about the disparity between what was said about the severity of the coronavirus in interviews with Bob Woodward and his efforts to "play it down" to the American people.

September 16, 2020

Michael Caputo, Assistant Secretary for Health and Human Services for Public Affairs, announces he will take a 60-day leave of absence after he accused government scientists of "sedition" and called on Trump's supporters to arm themselves ahead of the November 3rd election.

September 17, 2020

In austere, starkly divisive remarks, President Trump said he would create a commission to promote "patriotic education" and announced the creation of a grant to develop a "pro-American curriculum." The move is largely political — a reaction to a growing push by some academics for schools to teach an American history that better acknowledges slavery and systemic racism. The federal government does not have jurisdiction over school curriculum.

TRUMP: *Worst. President. Ever.*

September 18, 2020

The Centers for Disease Control and Prevention reverses a controversial guidance stating that asymptomatic people should not receive a COVID-19 test.

September 18, 2020

Associate Justice of the Supreme Court of the United States Ruth Bader Ginsburg passes away at age 87 due to pancreatic cancer.

September 19, 2020

President Trump addresses a crowd of supporters at a campaign rally in Fayetteville, North Carolina. During the rally he announces that he is planning on filling the vacant Supreme Court of the United States seat left by the death of Ruth Bader Ginsburg, pledging that he will nominate another woman.

September 21, 2020

Senior Judge of the United States District Court for the District of Nevada James C. Mahan dismisses a lawsuit filed by President Trump against the State of Nevada challenging the state's recent mail-in voting law.

September 23, 2020

President Trump holds a news conference in the James S. Brady Press Briefing Room. In response to a question about if he would commit to a peaceful transfer of power he says, "Well, we'll have to see what happens. You know that. I've been complaining very strongly about the ballots. And the ballots are a disaster,".

September 23, 2020

President Trump meets with multiple states Attorney Generals in the Cabinet Room of the White House, speaking on the "dangers of protecting Americans from censorship, cancel culture, and consumer abuses inflicted by big tech companies."

September 24, 2020

President Trump and First Lady Melania Trump pay respects to the late Justice Ruth Bader Ginsburg, who is lying in repose in the Great Hall of the United States Supreme Court Building. While paying their respects booing was heard from the crowd, as well as chants of "honor her wish".

September 25, 2020

Lucy Koh, United States District Judge of the Northern District of California, rules that the Trump Administration is not allowed to end the 2020 United States Census early, and orders the United States Census Bureau to continue through October 31st.

2020

September 29, 2020

President Trump and former Vice President Joe Biden participate in the first presidential debate at Case Western Reserve University in Cleveland, Ohio. The debate was widely criticized by commentators and journalists. It was called "a hot mess, inside a dumpster fire, inside a train wreck" and a "disgrace" (CNN's Jake Tapper); a "shitshow" (CNN's Dana Bash); "mud-wrestling" (ABC's Martha Raddatz); "the worst presidential debate I have ever seen in my life" (ABC's George Stephanopoulos); and "the single worst debate I have ever covered in my two decades of doing this job" (CNN's Chris Cillizza).

September 29, 2020

At one point during the debate, Biden and Wallace pressed Trump to condemn white supremacy groups. When Trump replied "Give me a name...", Biden responded with "The Proud Boys". Trump then said "Proud Boys, stand back and stand by, but I'll tell you what, I'll tell you what, somebody's got to do something about Antifa and the Left, because this is not a right-wing problem, this is a left-wing problem." This remark was interpreted by some members of that far-right group, as well as others, as a call to arms.

October 1, 2020

Hope Hicks, senior counselor to President Trump, tests positive for coronavirus. She traveled with President Trump to the debate in Cleveland on September 29 and to a rally in Minnesota on September 30.[1] Although some White House officials were aware of her diagnosis in the morning, "Trump still took a trip to New Jersey for a fundraiser, and press secretary Kayleigh McEnany still held a news briefing at the White House."

October 2, 2020

President Trump tweets that both he and First Lady Melania Trump had tested positive for coronavirus and would immediately quarantine. Later that day, President Trump boarded a helicopter to Walter Reed National Military Medical Center for treatment.

October 3, 2020

Senators Thom Tillis, Mike Lee and Ron Johnson all test positive for coronavirus. As a result, Senate Majority Leader Mitch McConnell halts all Senate floor action for two weeks.

October 4, 2020

After President Trump rides in a motorcade around Walter Reed Medical Center, a physician at the hospital says that every Secret Service agent inside the vehicle will have to quarantine for 14 days.

October 8, 2020

President Trump, having suddenly announced two days ago that he was ending negotiations with lawmakers regarding a new economic stimulus package, now says the talks are back on.

October 9, 2020

The Commission on Presidential Debates cancels the October 15 scheduled debate between the president and Joe Biden. President Trump had refused to participate virtually. The third and final debate remains scheduled for October 22.

October 16, 2020

The Federal Emergency Management Agency (FEMA) rejects California's request for federal aid for the on-going forest fires. A FEMA spokesperson remarked that the damage was "...not of such severity and magnitude to exceed the combined capabilities of the state, affected local governments, voluntary agencies and other responding federal agencies."

October 17, 2020

President Trump approves a federal disaster declaration for California's wildfires after having rejected the request the previous day.

October 25, 2020

CBS aired President Trump and Vice President Pence's interview for its news show 60 Minutes which was filmed earlier in the week. President Trump was perturbed at host Lesley Stahl asking "hard questions" and complained that former Vice President Biden had received "softball questions". Trump then walked off the set.

October 31, 2020

In his first speech after his hospitalization for Covid-19, President Donald Trump stood on a White House balcony on October 10 and made a grand declaration about the coronavirus: "It's going to disappear. It is disappearing.". 229,000 Americans have died to this point.

November 3, 2020

The 2020 United States presidential election is held. The interim results show President Trump carries 23 states and 213 electoral votes compared to former Vice President Joe Biden, who carries 20 states and leads 238 electoral votes. However, no winner is declared on election night with seven states still have not completed their vote counting. These states still being counted are Alaska, Georgia, Michigan, Nevada, North Carolina, Pennsylvania and Wisconsin.

November 4, 2020

Despite the lack of a clear winner, President Trump declares victory at approximately 2:00 a.m., claiming concerns about fraud and mail-in ballots.

TRUMP: *Worst. President. Ever.*

He states his intention to request that the Supreme Court prevent any more ballots from being counted.

....

November 5, 2020

President Trump holds a press conference in the White House. His opening statement is, "If you count the legal votes I easily win. If you count the illegal votes, they can try to steal the election from us." He continued, displaying misinterpretation of the Constitution, the role of the Supreme Court and the rule of law regarding the counting of votes. He did not take questions.

....

November 7, 2020

Former Vice President Joe Biden becomes president-elect after he had secured 290 electoral votes by winning Nevada and Pennsylvania, which he had reached over the required electoral votes of 270. However, President Trump refuses to concede defeat.

....

November 9, 2020

President Trump announces on Twitter that Secretary of Defense Mark Esper is fired and that Christopher C. Miller, Director of the National Counterterrorism, is nominated to replace him.

....

November 10, 2020

Secretary of State Mike Pompeo denied President-elect Joe Biden's success in the recent 2020 presidential election, declaring that "there will be a smooth transition to a second Trump administration."

....

November 12, 2020

The Cybersecurity and Infrastructure Security Agency, part of the Department of Homeland Security, reports that the 2020 presidential election was "the most secure in American history". The election officials also said they found "no evidence that any voting system deleted or lost votes, changed votes or was in any way compromised".

....

November 17, 2020

President Trump announces on Twitter that he is firing Director of the Cybersecurity and Infrastructure Security Agency (CISA) Chris Krebs for contradicting him on the prevalence of fraud in the recent presidential election.

....

November 19, 2020

After the Georgia recount is completed, President-elect Joe Biden is projected to win Georgia and its 16 electoral votes putting the total projected electoral votes to 306 for Biden and 232 for Trump. All states have now been called within 16 days after the election.

....

November 20, 2020

President Trump meets with two Republican legislative leaders from Michigan at the White House to discuss the possibility that the Michigan board of canvassers could choose to not to certify the election results. The state legislatures would then appoint different electors who would possibly overturn the will of the voters. However, the lawmakers reaffirmed that they would honor the results of the election in Michigan and stated that there is no reason to overturn the results.

November 22, 2020

President Trump again briefly participates in the virtual G20 summit in Riyadh and delivers a virtual address. Trump criticized the Paris Agreement and stated that it crippled the United States economy.

November 25, 2020

President Trump pardons former National Security Advisor Michael Flynn, who pleaded guilty to making false statements during the Mueller investigation in 2017.

November 26, 2020

President Trump admits that he will leave office if the electoral college votes for Joe Biden, adding it would be a mistake "and a very hard thing to concede".

December 3, 2020

President Trump uploads a 46-minute speech on his claims of alleged voter fraud to his social media platforms titled "This may be the most important speech I've ever made....".

December 5, 2020

President Trump holds a rally for Senators David Perdue and Kelly Loeffler in Valdosta, Georgia, and spends most of the 100 minute speech on his conspiratorial theories of electoral fraud rather than on the runoff elections against Raphael Warnock and Jon Ossoff, respectively.

December 9, 2020

Texas Attorney General Ken Paxton files an amicus brief with the Supreme Court asking to block four states — Pennsylvania, Michigan, Wisconsin, and Georgia — from casting electoral votes for President-elect Joe Biden.

December 9, 2020

President Trump hosts the annual White House Hanukkah Party and in a speech to guests claims he will be re-elected, despite losing the election, if the Supreme Court "[has] courage".

December 10, 2020

President Trump acknowledges that

there will be a Biden administration, admitting that he lost the election. He also called for the Supreme Court to follow the Constitution and "do what has to be done".

December 11, 2020

The Supreme Court declines to hear the Paxton lawsuit (seeking to overturn the 2020 presidential election) stating that the State of Texas did not have legal standing to bring the case before the Court.

December 14, 2020

All 538 electors for the electoral college met to cast their votes and finalize the 2020 election results. Both candidates received their projected counts of 306 for Biden and 232 for Trump without faithless electors.

December 14, 2020

Senate majority leader Mitch McConnell congratulates Joe Biden and Kamala Harris, accepting the results of the 2020 election in another blow to President Trump's attempt to delegitimise the election results, saying, "Many of us had hoped the presidential election would yield a different result" and that "all Americans can take pride that our nation has a female vice president-elect for the very first time".

December 18, 2020

The Trump administration announces they will close the remaining two U.S. consulates in Russia following a suspected cyberattack on government agencies.

December 22, 2020

President Trump announces that he may not sign the $900B COVID-19 relief bill, which was passed by both the House and Senate.

December 22, 2020

President Trump grants 20 high-profile pardons. Among them are 4 Blackwater guards convicted of 17 murders in 2007, 2 Border Patrol agents in prison for murder and several corrupt former politicians.

December 23, 2020

President Trump vetoes the National Defense Authorization Act for Fiscal Year 2021.

December 28, 2020

The House of Representatives votes 322—87 to override President Trump's veto of the National Defense Authorization Act for Fiscal Year 2021.

President does not hold such legal power.

January 1, 2021

The United States Senate votes 81–13 to override President Trump's veto of the National Defense Authorization Act for Fiscal Year 2021. This marks the first successful veto override of the Trump presidency.

January 3, 2021

A phone call between President Trump and Georgia Secretary of State, Brad Raffensperger is leaked showing Trump telling him the election was a fraud and demanding he find "11,780 votes, which is one more than we have." Raffensperger responds that the election results were correct and that Trump's data is wrong. Trump continued to claim voter fraud and said Raffensperger would be a "criminal" if he did not change the election results.

January 5, 2021

U.S. District Judge Mark Howard Cohen denies an emergency injunction from President Trump to decertify the 2020 United States presidential election results in Georgia calling the lawsuit "beyond unprecedented".

January 6, 2021

President Trump holds a rally in Washington DC to decry the certification of Joe Biden as the victor in the November election. He also calls on Vice President Mike Pence to reject the electoral votes, even though the Vice

January 6, 2021

The U.S. Capitol building is evacuated during the Electoral College results certification process after seditionists and insurrectionists broke the security barrier and stormed the building. Both Houses of Congress recess the Electoral College debate after the mob forced a lockdown of the building. Vice President Mike Pence was evacuated.

January 6, 2021

Democrat Jon Ossoff is declared winner of the final Senate runoff election defeating Republican David Perdue giving Republicans and the Democrat caucus a 50/50 split in the Senate during the first 2 years of the Biden administration with the tie-breaking vote going to Vice President-elect Kamala Harris.

January 7, 2021

Vice President Mike Pence declares Joe Biden the winner of the 2020 presidential election after certification of the electoral votes resumed in a joint session of Congress.

January 7, 2021

As a result of yesterday's Capitol Hill breach, President Trump was suspended from Facebook and Instagram until after

TRUMP: *Worst. President. Ever.*

Joe Biden's Inauguration for allegedly inciting the riot. He was also suspended from Twitter for 24 hours, with the suspension only being lifted if he deleted three Tweets that Twitter say violated their terms of service because they used the platform "for the purpose of manipulating or interfering in elections or other civic processes".

January 7, 2021

House Speaker Nancy Pelosi calls for President Trump to be removed from office by way of the 25th Amendment over his involvement in the storming of Capitol Hill and states impeachment proceedings will be started should this not happen.

January 7, 2021

For the first time, President Trump condemns the attack on the United States Capitol and concedes the race to Joe Biden. He also says that his focus is to ensure a smooth transition of power to the "next administration".

January 8, 2021

President Trump announces he will not be attending Joe Biden's inauguration making him the first outgoing President not to attend his successor's inauguration since the 1974 Inauguration of Gerald Ford.

January 8, 2021

President-elect Joe Biden calls President Trump's decision not to attend his inauguration "One of the few things he and I have ever agreed on. It's a good thing, him not showing up."

January 8, 2021

President Trump's personal Twitter account @realDonaldTrump is permanently suspended with Twitter citing "risk of further incitement of violence" following the storming of Capitol Hill which Twitter allege Trump incited.

January 10, 2021

Vice President Mike Pence announced he will be attending Joe Biden's Inauguration despite President Trump refusing to attend.

January 11, 2021

House Speaker Nancy Pelosi gives Vice President Mike Pence an ultimatum: Invoke the 25th Amendment within 24 hours to remove President Trump from office or they will begin Impeachment proceedings against the President.

TRUMP: *Worst. President. Ever.*

January 11, 2021

The Professional Golfer's Association announced the PGA Championship will no longer be taking place at President Trump's Golf course in New Jersey as they say it would be "detrimental to the brand".

January 11, 2021

Democrats in the House of Representatives formally charge President Trump with one count of "incitement of insurrection" after Republicans in the House block invocation of the 25th Amendment making Trump the first President to face two Impeachment trials.

January 11, 2021

President Trump and Vice President Pence speak for the first time since the storming of the Capitol.

January 12, 2021

Alex Azar announces that HHS will make changes to their vaccine distributions in an effort to speed up the rollout by encouraging states to open vaccination sites to all persons older than 65,[147] however at the time the announcement was made, stockpiles were already exhausted.

January 12, 2021

President Trump speaks publicly for the first time since his permanent Twitter ban and articles of Impeachment being drawn against him calling it a "continuation of the greatest witch hunt in political history" when speaking to reporters.

January 13, 2021

President Trump releases a statement calling for "no violence" in wakes of reports of planned armed demonstrations ahead of Biden's inauguration.

January 12, 2021

President Trump becomes the first president in U.S. history to be impeached twice after the House of Representatives voted yes to impeach Trump on the charge of "Incitement of insurrection". 222 Democrats and 10 Republicans voted yea while 197 Republicans voted nay with 4 Republicans not voting. He now faces trial at the Senate which will not take place until after his term has expired.

January 14, 2021

Vice President Mike Pence congratulates incoming Vice President Kamala Harris, 73 days after the presidential election.

January 18, 2021

First Lady Melania Trump delivers a farewell address, urging Americans to Be Best.

....

January 19, 2021

Acting Deputy Secretary of Homeland Security Ken Cuccinelli signs an agreement with the union representing ICE agents that essentially hands control of immigration policy to the union.

....

January 20, 2021

President Trump grants pardons to 73 individuals and commutes the sentence for 70 others prior to finishing his term.

....

January 20, 2021

Joe Biden is inaugurated the 46th president at noon EST. President Trump did not attend the ceremony and begins his post-presidency.

....

TRUMP: *Worst. President. Ever.*

Facts and Figures of the Trump Presidency

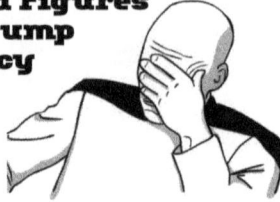

Donald Trump will go down in history as the first president with a net loss of U.S. jobs over a four-year term in federal tracking of the statistic that goes back to just after the Great Depression.

On a percentage basis, the biggest jobs gains over the last half-century were posted during Carter (12.8%), Reagan's second term (11.2%) and Clinton's second term (10.5%).

Donald Trump is the only president to be impeached twice.

Donald Trump had the highest White House staff turnover of any president.

45% of President Trump's "A Team" departures have undergone serial turnover as of January 20, 2021, higher than the last 4 presidents COMBINED.

President Trump's cabinet turned over more than the last 3 presidents combined, two of which served 8 years.

In four years, President Trump made 30,573 false or misleading claims, according to Washington Post fact-checkers.

PolitiFact awarded Trump its "Lie of the Year" in 2015, 2017 and 2019. In 2016, the winner was "Fake News", and 2020 was Covid-19 Downplay and Denial.

A full 26 incidents of "unwanted sexual contact" and 43 instances of inappropriate behaviour were detailed against Donald Trump.

A full 26 incidents of "unwanted sexual contact" and 43 instances of inappropriate behaviour were detailed against Donald Trump.

Trump suggested to Prime Minister Shinzo Abe of Japan during a meeting at Mar-a-Lago in February 2017 that Abe grant a coveted operating license to a casino company owned by Sheldon Adelson, who donated at least $20 million to Trump's presidential campaign.

Ben Carson, the housing and urban development secretary, let his son help organize an official department event and invite people with whom the son had potential business dealings.

Scott Pruitt, the former E.P.A. head, asked his staff members to contact Republicans donors with the goal of helping his wife find a job. Pruitt also rented a condo on Capitol Hill for $50 a night, well below market value, from the wife of an energy lobbyist whose project the E.P.A. approved last March. Pruitt's many scandals led to his resignation in July.

Elaine Chao, the transportation secretary, used interviews with Chinese and Chinese-American media to raise her father's profile. He is a shipping magnate whose business transports goods between the United States and Asia, and he sat next to her during the interviews.

And although it doesn't quite rise to the same level of the other examples here: White House staffers receive a discount of up to 70 percent on Trump-branded merchandise at the president's Bedminster, N.J., golf club, reportedly at the president's recommendation.

Mar-a-Lago, Donald Trump's private club, charged taxpayers $3 for every glass of water that was consumed there during the Trump presidency.

Eased restrictions on loan sharks;

Passed gigantic, regressive tax cuts designed to allow CEOs and shareholders to pay a lower rate on their passive income than workers did on their wages;

Exploded the deficit, from $585 billion to $3,700 billion year end 2020.

Sabotaged Obamacare. . The number of uninsured Americans rose by 2.3 million from 2016 to 2019, including 726,000 children.

Put a man on the Supreme Court who claimed accusations of sexual assault against him were engineered as "revenge on behalf of the Clintons," and another who said it should be legal to fire a trucker for abandoning his broken-down truck to get help rather than freezing to death;

Alienated foreign allies while cozying up to murderous autocrats;

Dragged the U.S. into a self-defeating trade war with China that caused layoffs and losses at American companies and was paid for by American taxpayers

Used the armed forces for a $200 million election stunt;

Proposed a plan to let coal plants regulate themselves that would kill up to 1,400 Americans annually;

Presided over a 17% rise in hate crimes in the year prior, including a 37% increase in anti-Semitic hate crimes;

Let Puerto Rico implode and smeared its dead

Ceded any moral high ground whatsoever when it came to condemning human rights abuses—not that he'd ever do anything like that—by letting his Saudi pals get away with killing a U.S. resident.

QUOTES

Quotes of the Trump Presidency

"I will build a great, great wall on our southern border, and I will have Mexico pay for that wall. Mark my words."

Campaign launch rally, 15/6/15

....

"I will be phenomenal to the women. I mean, I want to help women."

Face the Nation, 9/8/15

....

'I've said if Ivanka weren't my daughter, perhaps I'd be dating her."

....

In Trump's victory speech following the Nevada caucuses : "I love the poorly educated."

....

On the rich:
Trump decided to get frank about his decision to exclusively fill his Cabinet with cartoonishly rich robber baron-types. "Somebody said, 'Why did you appoint a rich person to be in charge of the economy?'" he told the crowd. And he explained, "'Because that's the kind of thinking we want. I love all people. Rich or poor. But in those particular positions, I just don't want a poor person. Does that make sense?'"

....

'You must go forth into the world, with passion, courage in your conviction, and most importantly be true to yourself. I did it!' – Ah onto one of Donald's most hilarious moments here. Who can forgot that time he gave a commencement speech at Liberty University in Lynchburg, Virginia, and was called out for copying Legally Blonde's Elle Wood's graduation speech?'"

....

"Why would Kim Jong-un insult me by calling me old, when I would never call him short and fat? Oh well, I try so hard to be his friend and maybe someday that will happen," he had tweeted.

....

"You have 2,000 miles. You have mountains, you have rivers, you have things that you don't put the wall in, you don't need them." — Interview with Fox News on Mexican wall.

....

"So the wall. The wall's never meant to be 2,100 miles long. We have mountains that are far better than a wall. We have violent rivers that nobody goes near. ...You don't need a wall where you have a natural barrier that's far greater than any wall you could build, O.K.?"— Interview with The Wall Street Journal.

....

'You know, it really doesn't matter what the media write as long as you've got a young, and beautiful, piece of ass.'

....

'You're disgusting.' – To put this into context, Donald Trump said this to the opposing lawyer during a court case when she asked for a medical break to

TRUMP: *Worst. President. Ever.*

pump breast milk for her three-month-old daughter.

....

On E. Jean Carroll's rape allegation:
Trump said: "I'll say it with great respect: Number one, she's not my type. Number two, it never happended..."
.

....

On Racism:
"I'm the least racist person you have ever interviewed."
14/1/18

Claiming that 15,000 Haitians who had obtained visas to live in the U.S. "all have AIDS" and that 40,000 Nigerian visa holders would never "go back to their huts"

Kicking off his candidacy for president by calling Mexicans "drug dealers," "rapists," and "criminals"

Calling white supremacists, neo-Nazis, and members of the KKK "some very fine people"

Asking a Black reporter to set up a meeting with the Congressional Black Caucus, because he apparently thinks all Black people are friends

Describing minority communities as "ghettos" where "gangs [roam] the streets"

Calling for the execution of the five Black, wrongfully accused teenagers

Spending a good portion of "executive time" targeting Black athletes and retweeting anti-Muslim hate videos from white nationalist accounts

Spending half a decade spreading a conspiracy theory that America's first Black president was not born in the United States

....

On the environement:
"I'm an environmentalist. A lot of people don't understand that. I think I know more about the environment than most people."

....

On global warming:
"I'm not a believer in man-made global warming. It could be warming, and it's going to start to cool at some point. And you know, in the early, in the 1920s, people talked about global cooling...They thought the Earth was cooling. Now, it's global warming...But the problem we have, and if you look at our energy costs, and all of the things that we're doing to solve a problem that I don't think in any major fashion exists."

....

"[Kim Jong-Un] speaks and his people sit up at attention. I want my people to do the same."

Fox & Friends, 15/6/18

....

Trump on death of ISIS leader Abu Bakr al-Baghdadi:
"Baghdadi has been on the run for many years, long before I took office. But at my direction, as commander-in-chief of the United States, we obliterated his caliphate, 100%, in March of this year."

....

On coronavirus:
"We have it totally under control. It's one person coming in from China. It's going to be just fine."

TRUMP: *Worst. President. Ever.*

QUOTES

....

On Health Care:
"Nobody knew health care could be so complicated."

Washington Post, 27/2/17

....

On Winning Graciously:
"Crooked Hillary Clinton is the worst (and biggest) loser of all time. She just can't stop, which is so good for the Republican Party. Hillary, get on with your life and give it another try in three years!"

Twitter, 18/11/17

....

On Russia:
"Russia will have much greater respect for our country when I am leading it than when other people have led it...If Putin likes Donald Trump, I consider that an asset, not a liability, because we have a horrible relationship with Russia."

Trump Tower Press Conference, 11/1/17

....

November 4, 2020 "We are up BIG, but they are trying to STEAL the Election. We will never let them do it. Votes cannot be cast after the Polls are closed!"

....

"I could stand in the middle of 5th Avenue and shoot somebody and I wouldn't lose voters."

23/1/16

....

TRUMP: *Worst. President. Ever.*

TRUMP: *Worst. President. Ever.*

EPILOGUE

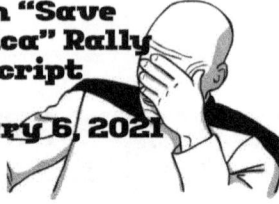

Donald Trump Speech "Save America" Rally Transcript

January 6, 2021

This is the speech that President Trump gave in Washington, D.C. to rally his supporters. Afterwards, these supporters attacked the U.S. Capitol, the first time since the War of 1812. As a result, 5 people were killed, including a U.S. Capital policeman.

Donald Trump: (Beginning)
The media will not show the magnitude of this crowd. Even I, when I turned on today, I looked, and I saw thousands of people here, but you don't see hundreds of thousands of people behind you because they don't want to show that. We have hundreds of thousands of people here, and I just want them to be recognized by the fake news media. Turn your cameras please and show what's really happening out here because these people are not going to take it any longer. They're not going to take it any longer. Go ahead. Turn your cameras, please. Would you show? They came from all over the world, actually, but they came from all over our country. I just really want to see what they do. I just want to see how they covered. I've never seen anything like it. But it would be really great if we could be covered fairly by the media. The media is the biggest problem we have as far as I'm concerned, single biggest problem, the fake news and the big tech. Big tech is now coming into their own. We beat them four years ago. We surprised them. We took them by surprise and this year, they rigged an election. They rigged it like they've never rigged an election before. By the way, last night, they didn't do a bad job either, if

you notice. I'm honest. I just, again, I want to thank you. It's just a great honor to have this kind of crowd and to be before you. Hundreds of thousands of American patriots are committed to the honesty of our elections and the integrity of our glorious Republic. All of us here today do not want to see our election victory stolen by emboldened radical left Democrats, which is what they're doing and stolen by the fake news media. That's what they've done and what they're doing. We will never give up. We will never concede, it doesn't happen. You don't concede when there's theft involved.

Donald Trump: (04:42)
Our country has had enough. We will not take it anymore and that's what this is all about. To use a favorite term that all of you people really came up with, we will stop the steal. Today I will lay out just some of the evidence proving that we won this election, and we won it by a landslide. This was not a close election. I say sometimes jokingly, but there's no joke about it, I've been in two elections. I won them both and the second one, I won much bigger than the first. Almost 75 million people voted for our campaign, the most of any incumbent president by far in the history of our country, 12 million more people than four years ago. I was told by the real pollsters, we do have real pollsters. They know that we were going to do well, and we were going to win. What I was told, if I went from 63 million, which we had four years ago to 66 million, there was no chance of losing. Well, we didn't go to 66. We went to 75 million and they say we lost. We didn't lose.

Donald Trump: (06:08)
By the way, does anybody believe that Joe had 80 million votes? Does anybody believe that? He had 80 million computer votes. It's a disgrace. There's never been anything like that. You could take third world countries. Just take a look, take

TRUMP: *Worst. President. Ever.*

third world countries. Their elections are more honest than what we've been going through in this country. It's a disgrace. It's a disgrace. Even when you look at last night, they're all running around like chickens with their heads cut off with boxes. Nobody knows what the hell is going on. There's never been anything like this. We will not let them silence your voices. We're not going to let it happen. Not going to let it happen.

Crowd: (07:11)
Fight for Trump! Fight for Trump! Fight for Trump!

Donald Trump: (07:11)
Thank you. I'd love to have, if those tens of thousands of people would be allowed, the military, the secret service, and we want to thank you, and the police law enforcement. Great. You're doing a great job, but I'd love it if they could be allowed to come up here with us. Is that possible? Can you just let them come up, please? Rudy, you did a great job. He's got guts. You know what? He's got guts, unlike a lot of people in the Republican party. He's got guts, he fights. He fights, and I'll tell you. Thank you very much, John. Fantastic job. I watched. That's a tough act to follow, those two. John is one of the most brilliant lawyers in the country, and he looked at this and he said, " What an absolute disgrace, that this could be happening to our constitution." He looked at Mike Pence, and I hope Mike is going to do the right thing.

Donald Trump: (08:09)
I hope so. I hope so because if Mike Pence does the right thing, we win the election. All he has to do. This is from the number one or certainly one of the top constitutional lawyers in our country. He has the absolute right to do it. We're supposed to protect our country, support our country, support our constitution, and protect our constitution. States want to revote. The States got defrauded. They were given false information. They voted on it. Now they want to recertify. They want it back. All Vice-President Pence has to do is send it back to the States to recertify, and we become president, and you are the happiest people.

Donald Trump: (09:08)
I just spoke to Mike. I said, "Mike, that doesn't take courage. What takes courage is to do nothing. That takes courage," and then we're stuck with a president who lost the election by a lot, and we have to live with that for four more years. We're just not going to let that happen. Many of you have traveled from all across the nation to be here, and I want to thank you for the extraordinary love. That's what it is. There's never been a movement like this ever, ever for the extraordinary love for this amazing country and this amazing movement. Thank you.

Crowd: (09:44)
We love Trump! We love Trump! We love Trump!

Donald Trump: (09:59)
By the way, this goes all the way back past the Washington monument. Do you believe this? Look at this. Unfortunately, they gave the press the prime seats. I can't stand that. No, but you look at that behind. I wish they'd flip those cameras and look behind you. That is the most amazing sight. When they make a mistake, you get to see it on television. Amazing, amazing, all the way back. Don't worry. We will not take the name off the Washington monument. We will not. Cancel culture. They wanted to get rid of the Jefferson Memorial, either take it down or just put somebody else in there. I don't think that's going to happen. It damn well better not. Although with this administration, if this happens, it could happen. You'll see some really bad things happen.

Donald Trump: (10:54)
They'll knock out Lincoln too, by the way. They've been taking his statue down, but

then we signed a little law. You hurt our monuments, you hurt our heroes, you go to jail for 10 years and everything stopped. Did you notice that? It stopped. It all stopped. They could use Rudy back in New York City. Rudy, they could use you. Your city is going to hell. They want Rudy Giuliani back in New York. We'll get a little younger version of Rudy. Is that okay, Rudy?

Donald Trump: (11:25)
We're gathered together in the heart of our nation's Capitol for one very, very basic and simple reason, to save our democracy. Most candidates on election evening, and of course this thing goes on so long, they still don't have any idea what the votes are. We still have congressional seats under review. They have no idea. They've totally lost control. They've used the pandemic as a way of defrauding the people in a proper election. But when you see this and when you see what's happening, number one, they all say, "Sir, we'll never let it happen again." I said, "That's good, but what about eight weeks ago?" They try and get you to go. They say, "Sir, in four years, you're guaranteed." I said, "I'm not interested right now. Do me a favor, go back eight weeks. I want to go back eight weeks. Let's go back eight week." We want to go back, and we want to get this right because we're going to have somebody in there that should not be in there and our country will be destroyed, and we're not going to stand for that.

Donald Trump: (12:34)
For years, Democrats have gotten away with election fraud and weak Republicans, and that's what they are. There's so many weak Republicans. We have great ones, Jim Jordan, and some of these guys. They're out there fighting the House. Guys are fighting, but it's incredible. Many of the Republicans, I helped them get in. I helped them get elected. I helped Mitch get elected. I could name 24 of them, let's say. I won't bore

you with it, and then all of a sudden you have something like this. It's like, "Gee, maybe I'll talk to the president sometime later." No, it's amazing. The weak Republicans, they're pathetic Republicans and that's what happens. If this happened to the Democrats, there'd be hell all over the country going on. There'd be hell all over the country. But just remember this. You're stronger, you're smarter. You've got more going than anybody, and they try and demean everybody having to do with us, and you're the real people. You're the people that built this nation. You're not the people that tore down our nation.

Donald Trump: (13:45)
The weak Republicans, and that's it. I really believe it. I think I'm going to use the term, the weak Republicans. You got a lot of them, and you got a lot of great ones, but you got a lot of weak ones. They've turned a blind eye even as Democrats enacted policies that chipped away our jobs, weakened our military, threw open our borders and put America last. Did you see the other day where Joe Biden said, "I want to get rid of the America first policy." What's that all about, get rid of ...? How do you say, "I want to get rid of America first?" Even if you're going to do it, don't talk about it. Unbelievable, what we have to go through, what we have to go through and you have to get your people to fight. If they don't fight, we have to primary the hell out of the ones that don't fight. You primary them. We're going to let you know who they are. I can already tell you, frankly.

Donald Trump: (14:39)
But this year using the pretext of the China virus and the scam of mail-in ballots, Democrats attempted the most brazen and outrageous election theft. There's never been anything like this. It's a pure theft in American history, everybody knows it. That election, our election was over at 10:00 in the evening. We're leading Pennsylvania, Michigan,

Georgia by hundreds of thousands of votes, and then late in the evening or early in the morning, boom, these explosions of and bullshit, and all of a sudden. All of a sudden it started to happen.

Donald Trump: (15:35)
Don't forget when Romney got beat. Romney. I wonder if he enjoyed his flight in last night? But when Romney got beaten, he stands up like you're more typical. Well, I'd like to congratulate the victor, the victor. Who was the victor, Mitt? I'd like to congratulate. They don't go and look at the facts. Now I don't know. He got slaughtered probably, maybe it was okay. Maybe it was that's what happened. But we look at the facts and our lecture was so corrupt that in the history of this country, we've never seen anything like it. You can go all the way back. America is blessed with elections all over the world. They talk about our elections. You know what the world says about us now? They said we don't have free and fair elections and you know what else? We don't have a free and fair press.

Donald Trump: (16:25)
Our media is not free. It's not fair. It suppresses thought. It suppresses speech, and it's become the enemy of the people. It's become the enemy of the people. It's the biggest problem we have in this country. No third world countries would even attempt to do what we caught them doing and you'll hear about that in just a few minutes. Republicans are constantly fighting like a boxer with his hands tied behind his back. It's like a boxer, and we want to be so nice. We want to be so respectful of everybody, including bad people. We're going to have to fight much harder and Mike Pence is going to have to come through for us. If he doesn't, that will be a sad day for our country because you're sworn to uphold our constitution. Now it is up to Congress to confront this egregious assault on our democracy.

After this, we're going to walk down and I'll be there with you. We're going to walk down. We're going to walk down any one you want, but I think right here. We're going walk down to the Capitol, and we're going to cheer on our brave senators, and congressmen and women. We're probably not going to be cheering so much for some of them because you'll never take back our country with weakness. You have to show strength, and you have to be strong.

Donald Trump: (18:16)
We have come to demand that Congress do the right thing and only count the electors who have been lawfully slated, lawfully slated. I know that everyone here will soon be marching over to the Capitol building to peacefully and patriotically make your voices heard. Today we will see whether Republicans stand strong for integrity of our elections, but whether or not they stand strong for our country, our country. Our country has been under siege for a long time, far longer than this four-year period. We've set it on a much straighter course, a much ... I thought four more years. I thought it would be easy. We created-

Donald Trump: (19:03)
Four more years, I thought it would be easy. We created the greatest economy in history. We rebuilt our military. We get you the biggest tax cuts in history. We got you the biggest regulation cuts. There's no President, whether it's four years, eight years, or in one case more, got anywhere near the regulation cuts. It used to take 20 years to get a highway approved. now we're down to two. I want to get it down to one, but we're down to two. And it may get rejected for environmental or safety reasons, but we got it down the safety. We created Space Force. Look at what we did. Our military has been totally rebuilt. So we create Space Force, which by in of itself is a major achievement for an administration. And with us, it's one of so many different

things.

Donald Trump: (19:52)
Right to try. Everybody know about right to try. We did things that nobody ever thought possible. We took care of our vets. Our vets, the VA now has the highest rating, 91%, the highest rating that it's had from the beginning, 91% approval rating. Always you watch the VA, when it was on television. Every night people living in a horrible, horrible manner. We got that done. We got accountability done. We got it so that now in the VA, you don't have to wait for four weeks, six weeks, eight weeks, four months to see a doctor. If you can't get a doctor, you go outside you get the doctor, you have them taken care of. And we pay the doctor. And we've not only made life wonderful for so many people, we've saved tremendous amounts of money, far secondarily, but we've saved a lot of money.

Donald Trump: (20:49)
And now we have the right to fire bad people in the VA. We had 9000 people that treated our veterans horribly. In primetime, they would not have treated our veterans badly. But they treated our veterans horribly. And we have what's called the VA Accountability Act. And the accountability says if we see somebody in there that doesn't treat our vets well, or they steal, they rob, they do things badly. We say, "Joe, you're fired. Get out of here." Before you couldn't do that. You couldn't do that before.

Donald Trump: (21:24)
So we've taken care of things. We've done things like nobody's ever thought possible. And that's part of the reason that many people don't like us, because we've done too much, but we've done it quickly. And we were going to sit home and watch a big victory. And everybody had us down for a victory. It was going to be great. And now we're out here fighting. I said to somebody, I was going to take a few days and relax after our big electoral victory. Ten o'clock, it was over. But I was going to take a few days.

Donald Trump: (21:52)
And I can say this, since our election, I believe, which was a catastrophe when I watch and even these guys knew what happened, they know what happened. They're saying, "Wow, Pennsylvania's insurmountable. Wow, Wisconsin, look at the big leads we had." Even though the press said we were going to lose Wisconsin by 17 points. Even though press said Ohio is going to be close, we set a record. Florida's going to be close, we set a record. Texas is going to be close. Texas is going to be close, we set a record. And we set a record with Hispanic, with the Black community. We set a record with everybody.

Donald Trump: (22:36)
Today, we see a very important event though, because right over there, right there, we see the event going to take place. And I'm going to be watching, because history is going to be made. We're going to see whether or not we have great and courageous leaders or whether or not we have leaders that should be ashamed of themselves throughout history, throughout eternity, they'll be ashamed. And you know what? If they do the wrong thing, we should never ever forget that they did. Never forget. We should never ever forget. With only three of the seven states in question, we win the presidency of the United States.

Donald Trump: (23:21)
And by the way, it's much more important today than it was 24 hours ago. Because I spoke to David Perdue, what a great person, and Kelly Loeffler, two great people, but it was a setup. And I said, "We have no back line anymore." The only back line, the only line of demarcation, the only line that we have is the veto of the president of the United States. So this is now what we're doing, a far more

TRUMP: *Worst. President. Ever.*

important election than it was two days ago.

Donald Trump: (23:59)
I want to thank the more than 140 members of the House. Those are warriors. They're over there working like you've never seen before, studying, talking, actually going all the way back, studying the roots of the Constitution, because they know we have the right to send a bad vote that was illegally got, they gave these people bad things to vote for and they voted, because what did they know? And then when they found out a few weeks later... Again, it took them four years to devise history. And the only unhappy person in the United States, single most unhappy, is Hillary Clinton because she said, "Why didn't you do this for me four years ago? Why didn't you do this for me four years ago? Change the votes! 10,000 in Michigan. You could have changed the whole thing!" But she's not too happy. You notice you don't see her anymore. What happened? Where is Hillary? Where is she?

Donald Trump: (24:57)
But I want to thank all of those congressmen and women. I also want to thank our 13 most courageous members of the US Senate, Senator Ted Cruz, Senator Ron Johnson, Senator Shadowless, Kelly Loeffler. And Kelly Loeffler, I'll tell you, she's been so great. She works so hard. So let's give her and David a little special head, because it was rigged against them. Let's give her and David. Kelly Loeffler, David Perdue. They fought a good race. They never had a shot. That equipment should never have been allowed to be used, and I was telling these people don't let them use this stuff. Marsha Blackburn, terrific person. Mike Braun, Indiana. Disinvested, great guy. Bill Hagerty, John Kennedy, James Lankford, Cynthia Lummis. Tommy Tuberville, to the coach. And Roger Marshall. We want to thank them, senators that stepped up, we want to thank them.

Donald Trump: (26:04)
I actually think though it takes, again, more courage not to step up. And I think a lot of those people are going to find that out, and you better start looking at your leadership because the leadership has led you down the tubes. "We don't want to give $2000 to people. We want to give them $600." Oh, great. How does that play politically? Pretty good? And this has nothing to do with politics. But how does it play politically? China destroyed these people. We didn't destroy. China destroyed them, totally destroyed them. We want to give them $600, and they just wouldn't change. I said, "Give them $2000. We'll pay it back. We'll pay it back fast. You already owe 26 trillion. Give them a couple of bucks. Let them live. Give them a couple of bucks!"

Donald Trump: (26:57)
And some of the people here disagree with me on that. But I just say, look, you got to let people live. And how does that play though? Okay, number one, it's the right thing to do. But how does that play politically? I think it's the primary reason, one of the primary reasons, the other was just pure cheating. That was the super primary reason. But you can't do that. You got to use your head.

Donald Trump: (27:19)
As you know the media is constantly asserted the outrageous lie that there was no evidence of widespread fraud. You ever see these people? "While there is no evidence of fraud..." Oh, really? Well, I'm going to read you pages. I hope you don't get bored listening to it. Promise? Don't get bored listening to it, all those hundreds of thousands of people back there. Move them up, please. Yeah. All these people don't get bored. Don't get angry at me because you're going to get bored because it's so much. The American people do not believe the corrupt fake news anymore. They have

TRUMP: *Worst. President. Ever.*   105

ruined their reputation.

Donald Trump: (27:57)
But it used to be that they'd argue with me, I'd fight. So I'd fight, they'd fight. I'd fight, they'd fight. Boop-boop. You'd believe me, you'd believe them. Somebody comes out. They had their point of view, I had my point of view. But you'd have an argument. Now what they do is they go silent. It's called suppression. And that's what happens in a communist country. That's what they do. They suppress. You don't fight with them anymore, unless it's a bad. They have a little bad story about me, they'll make it 10 times worse and it's a major headline. But Hunter Biden, they don't talk about him. What happened to Hunter? Where's Hunter? Where is Hunter? They don't talk about him.

Donald Trump: (28:34)
Now watch all the sets will go off. Well, they can't do that because they get good ratings. The ratings are too good. Now where is Hunter? And how come Joe was allowed to give a billion dollars of money to get rid of the prosecutor in Ukraine? How does that happen? I'd ask you that question. How does that happen? Can you imagine if I said that? If I said that it would be a whole different ball game. And how come Hunter gets three and a half million dollars from the Mayor of Moscow's wife, and gets hundreds of thousands of dollars to sit on an energy board even though he admits he has no knowledge of energy, and millions of dollars up front, and how come they go into China and they leave with billions of dollars to manage? "Have you managed money before?" "No, I haven't." "Oh, that's good. Here's about 3 billion."

Donald Trump: (29:29)
No, they don't talk about that. No, we have a corrupt media. They've gone silent. They've gone dead. I now realize how good it was if you go back 10 years. I realized how good, even though I didn't

necessarily love him, I realized how good it was like a cleansing motion. But we don't have that anymore. We don't have a fair media anymore. It's suppression and you have to be very careful with that. And they've lost all credibility in this country. We will not be intimidated into accepting the hoaxes and the lies that we've been forced to believe over the past several weeks. We've amassed overwhelming evidence about a fake election. This is the presidential election. Last night was a little bit better because of the fact that we had a lot of eyes watching one specific state, but they cheated like hell anyway.

Donald Trump: (30:27)
You have one of the dumbest governors in the United States. And when I endorsed him, I didn't know this guy. At the request of David Perdue. He said, "A friend of mine is running for Governor, what's his name." And you know the rest. He was in fourth place, fifth place. I don't know. He was way... He was doing poorly. I endorsed him. He went like a rocket ship and he won. And then I had to beat Stacey Abrams with this guy, Brian Kemp. I had to beat Stacey Abrams and I had to beat Oprah, used to be a friend of mine. I was on her last show. Her last week she picked the five outstanding people. I don't think she thinks that anymore. Once I ran for president, I didn't notice there were too many calls coming in from Oprah. Believe it or not, she used to like me, but I was one of the five outstanding people.

Donald Trump: (31:17)
And I had a campaign against Michelle Obama and Barack Hussein Obama against Stacey. And I had Brian Kemp, he weighs 130 pounds. He said he played offensive line in football. I'm trying to figure that. I'm still trying to figure that out. He said that the other night, "I was an offensive lineman." I'm saying, "Really? That must've been a really small team." But I look at that and I look at what's happened, and he turned out to be a

disaster. This stuff happens.

Donald Trump: (31:50)
Look, I'm not happy with the Supreme Court. They love to rule against me. I picked three people. I fought like hell for them, one in particular I fought. They all said, "Sir, cut him loose. He's killing us." The senators, very loyal senators. They're very loyal people. "Sir, cut him loose. He's killing us, sir. Cut him loose, sir." I must've gotten half of the senators. I said, "No, I can't do that. It's unfair to him. And it's unfair to the family. He didn't do anything wrong. They're made up stories." They were all made up stories. He didn't do anything wrong. "Cut him loose, sir." I said, "No, I won't do that." We got him through. And you know what? They couldn't give a damn. They couldn't give a damn. Let them rule the right way, but it almost seems that they're all going out of their way to hurt all of us, and to hurt our country. To hurt our country.

Donald Trump: (32:40)
I read a story in one of the newspapers recently how I control the three Supreme Court justices. I control them. They're puppets. I read it about Bill Barr, that he's my personal attorney. That he'll do anything for me. And I said, "It really is genius," because what they do is that, and it makes it really impossible for them to ever give you a victory, because all of a sudden Bill Barr changed, if you hadn't noticed. I like Bill Barr, but he changed, because he didn't want to be considered my personal attorney. And the Supreme Court, they rule against me so much. You know why? Because the story is I haven't spoken to any of them, any of them, since virtually they got in. But the story is that they're my puppet. That they're puppets. And now that the only way they can get out of that, because they hate that, it's not good on the social circuit. And the only way they get out is to rule against Trump. So let's rule against Trump, and they do that. So I want to congratulate them.

Donald Trump: (33:41)
But it shows you the media's genius. In fact, probably, if I was the media, I'd do it the same way. I hate to say it. But we got to get them straightened out. Today, for the sake of our democracy, for the sake of our Constitution, and for the sake of our children, we lay out the case for the entire world to hear. You want to hear it?

Crowd: (34:04)
Yes!

Donald Trump: (34:06)
In every single swing state, local officials, state officials, almost all Democrats made illegal and unconstitutional changes to election procedures without the mandated approvals by the state legislatures, that these changes paved the way for fraud on a scale never seen before. And I think we'd go a long way outside of our country when I say that.

Donald Trump: (34:34)
So just in a nutshell, you can't make a change on voting for a federal election unless the state legislature approves it. No judge can do it. Nobody can do it, only a legislature. So as an example in Pennsylvania or whatever, you have a Republican legislature, you have a Democrat mayor, and you have a lot of Democrats all over the place. They go to the legislature, the legislature laughs at them. Says, "We're not going to do that." They say, "Thank you very much." And they go and make the changes themselves. They do it anyway. And that's totally illegal. That's totally illegal. You can't do that.

Donald Trump: (35:13)
In Pennsylvania, the Democrat Secretary of State and the Democrat State Supreme Court justices illegally abolished the signature verification requirements just 11 days prior to the election. So think of what they did. No longer is there signature verification. Oh, that's okay. We

want voter ID by the way. But no longer is their signature verification, 11 days before the election! They say, "We don't want it." You know why they don't want it? Because they want to cheat. That's the only reason. Who would even think of that? We don't want to verify a signature? There were over 205,000 more ballots counted in Pennsylvania. Now think of this. You had 205,000 more ballots than you had voters. That means you had 200... Where did they come from? You know where they came from? Somebody's imagination. Whatever they needed. So in Pennsylvania you had 205,000 more votes than you had voters! And it's the number is actually much greater than that now. That was as of a week ago. And this is a mathematical impossibility, unless you want to say it's a total fraud. So Pennsylvania was defrauded.

Donald Trump: (36:35)
Over 8000 ballots in Pennsylvania were cast by people whose names and dates of birth match individuals who died in 2020 and prior to the election. Think of that. Dead people! Lots of dead people, thousands. And some dead people actually requested an application. That bothers me even more. Not only are they voting, they want an application to vote. One of them was 29 years ago died. It's incredible.

Donald Trump: (37:05)
Over 14,000 ballots were cast by out-of-state voters. So these are voters that don't live in the state. And by the way, these numbers are what they call outcome determinative. Meaning these numbers far surpass... I lost by a very little bit. These numbers are massive. Massive. More than 10,000 votes in Pennsylvania were illegally counted, even though they were received after Election Day. In other words, "They were received after Election Day, let's count them anyway!" And what they did in many cases is they did fraud. They took the date

and they moved it back, so that it no longer is after Election Day. And more than 60,000 ballots in Pennsylvania were reported received back. They got back before they were ever supposedly mailed out. In other words, you got the ballot back before you mailed it!

Donald Trump: (38:03)
... they were supposedly mailed out, in other words, you got the ballot back before you mailed it, which is also logically and logistically impossible. Think of that one. You got the ballot back. Let's send the ballots. Oh, they've already been sent. But we got the ballot back before they were sent. I don't think that's too good.

Donald Trump: (38:23)
Twenty-five thousand ballots in Pennsylvania were requested by nursing home residents, all in a single giant batch, not legal. Indicating an enormous illegal ballot harvesting operation. You're not allowed to do it. It's against the law. The day before the election, the State of Pennsylvania reported the number of absentee ballots that had been sent out. Yet this number was suddenly and drastically increased by 400,000 people. It was increased. Nobody knows where it came from by 400,000 ballots. One day after the election, it remains totally unexplained. They said, "Well, we can't figure that." Now that's many, many times what it would take to overthrow the state. Just that one element. 400,000 ballots appeared from nowhere, right after the election.

Donald Trump: (39:16)
By the way, Pennsylvania has now seen all of this. They didn't know because it was so quick. They had a vote, they voted, but now they see all this stuff. It's all come to light. Doesn't happen that fast. And they want to re certify their votes. They want to re certify. But the only way that can happen is if Mike Pence agrees to send it back.

Donald Trump: (39:43)
Mike Pence has to agree to send it back. And many people in Congress want it sent back, and take of what you're doing. Let's say you don't do it. Somebody says, "Well, we have to obey the constitution." And you are, because you're protecting our country and you're protecting the constitution, so you are. But think of what happens. Let's say they're stiffs and they're stupid people. And they say, "Well, we really have no choice." Even though Pennsylvania and other states want to redo their votes, they want to see the numbers. They already have the numbers. Go very quickly and they want to redo their legislature because many of these votes were taken as I said, because it wasn't approved by their legislature. That in itself is illegal and then you have the scam and that's all of the things that we're talking about. But think of this: if you don't do that, that means you will have a president of the United States for four years, with his wonderful son.

Donald Trump: (40:50)
You will have a president who lost all of these states, or you will have a president to put it another way, who was voted on by a bunch of stupid people who lost all of these things. You will have an illegitimate president, that's what you'll have. And we can't let that happen. These are the facts that you won't hear from the fake news media. It's all part of the suppression effort. They don't want to talk about it. They don't want to talk about it. In fact, when I started talking about that, I guarantee you a lot of the television sets and a lot of those cameras went off and that's how a lot of cameras back there. But a lot of them went off, but these are the things you don't hear about. You don't hear what you just heard. And I'm going to go over a few more states. But you don't hear it by the people who want to deceive you and demoralize you and control you, big tech, media.

Donald Trump: (41:48)
Just like the suppression polls that said, we're going to lose Wisconsin by 17 points, well we won Wisconsin. They don't have it that way because they lose just by a little sliver. But they had me down the day before Washington Post, ABC poll, down 17 points. I called up a real pollster. I said, "What is that?" "Sir, that's called a suppression poll. I think you're going to win Wisconsin, sir." I said, "But why do they make it four or five points?" "Because then people vote. But when you're down 17, they say, 'Hey, I'm not going to waste my time. I love the president, but there's no way.'" Despite that, we won Wisconsin, you'll see. But that's called suppression because a lot of people, when they see that, it's very interesting. This pollster said, "Sir, if you're down three, four or five people vote. When you go down 17, they say, 'Let's save, let's go and have dinner, and let's watch the presidential defeat tonight on television darling.'"

Donald Trump: (42:49)
And just like the radical left tries to blacklist you on social media, every time I put out a tweet, even if it's totally correct, totally correct. I get a flag. I get a flag. And they also don't let you get out. On Twitter, it's very hard to come on to my account. It's very hard to get out a message. They don't let the message get out nearly like they should, but I've had many people say, "I can't get on your Twitter." I don't care about Twitter. Twitter is bad news. They're all bad news. But you know what? If you want to get out of message. And if you want to go through big tech, social media, they are really, if you're a conservative, if you're a Republican, if you have a big voice, I guess they call it shadow ban. Shadow ban. They shadow ban you and it should be illegal. I've been telling these Republicans get rid of Section 230.

Donald Trump: (43:47)
And for some reason, Mitch and the

group, they don't want to put it in there. And they don't realize that that's going to be the end of the Republican party as we know it, but it's never going to be the end of us, never. Let them get out. Let the weak ones get out. This is a time for strength. They also want to indoctrinate your children in school by teaching them things that aren't so. They want to indoctrinate your children. It's all part of the comprehensive assault on our democracy and the American people to finally standing up and saying, "No." This crowd is again a testament to it. I did no advertising. I did nothing. You do have some groups that are big supporters. I want to thank that Amy and everybody, we have some incredible supporters, incredible, but we didn't do anything. This just happened.

Donald Trump: (44:39)
Two months ago, we had a massive crowd come down to Washington. I said, "What are they there for." "Sir, they're there for you." We have nothing to do with it. These groups, they're forming all over the United States. And we got to remember, in a year from now, you're going to start working on Congress. And we got to get rid of the weak congresspeople, the ones that aren't any good, the Liz Cheneys of the world, we got to get rid of them. We got to get rid of them. She never wants a soldier brought home. I've brought a lot of our soldiers home. I don't know, some like it. They're in countries that nobody even knows the name. Nobody knows where they are. They're dying. They're great, but they're dying. They're losing their arms, their legs, their face. I brought them back home, largely back home, Afghanistan, Iraq. Remember I used to say in the old days, "Don't go into Iraq. But if you go in, keep the oil." We didn't keep the oil. So stupid. So stupid, these people. And Iraq has billions and billions of dollars now in the bank. And what did we do? We get nothing. We never get. But we do actually, we kept the oil here. We did good. We got

rid of the ISIS caliphate. We got rid of plenty of different things that everybody knows and the rebuilding of our military in three years, people said it couldn't be done. And it was all made in the USA, all made in the USA. Best equipment in the world. In Wisconsin, corrupt Democrat run cities deployed more than 500 illegal unmanned, unsecured drop boxes, which collected a minimum of 91,000 unlawful votes. It was razor thin the loss. This one thing alone is much more than we would need, but there are many things.

Donald Trump: (46:29)
They have these lockboxes and they pick them up and they disappear for two days. People would say, "Where's that box?" They disappeared. Nobody even knew where the hell it was. In addition, over 170,000 absentee votes were counted in Wisconsin without a valid absentee ballot application. So they had a vote, but they had no application. And that's illegal in Wisconsin. Meaning those votes were blatantly done in opposition to state law. And they came 100% from Democrat areas, such as Milwaukee and Madison, 100%. In Madison, 17,000 votes were deposited in so-called human drop boxes. You know what that is, right? Where operatives stuff thousands of unsecured ballots into duffel bags on park benches across the city in complete defiance of cease and desist letters from state legislature. The state legislature said, "Don't do it." They're the only ones that could approve it. They gave tens of thousands of votes.

Donald Trump: (47:37)
They came in in duffel bags. Where the hell did they come from? According to eyewitness testimony, postal service workers in Wisconsin were also instructed to illegally backdate approximately 100,000 ballots. The margin of difference in Wisconsin was less than 20,000 votes. Each one of these things alone wins us the state. Great state, we love the state, we won the state. In

Georgia, your secretary of state, I can't believe this guy's a Republican. He loves recording telephone conversations. I thought it was a great conversation personally, so did a lot of other ... people love that conversation, because it says what's going on. These people are crooked. They're 100% in my opinion, one of the most corrupt. Between your governor and your secretary of state. And now you have it again last night, just take a look at what happened, what a mess and the Democrat party operatives entered into an illegal and unconstitutional settlement agreement that drastically weakened signature verification and other election security procedures.

Donald Trump: (48:53)
Stacey Abrams, she took them to lunch and I beat her two years ago with a bad candidate, Brian Kemp. But the Democrats, took the Republicans to lunch because the secretary of state had no clue what the hell was happening, unless he did have a clue. That's interesting. Maybe he was with the other side, but we've been trying to get verifications of signatures in Fulton County. They won't let us do it. The only reason they won't is because we'll find things in the hundreds of thousands. Why wouldn't they let us verify signatures and Fulton County? Which is known for being very corrupt. They won't do it. They go to some other county where you would live. I said, "That's not the problem. The problem is Fulton County." Home of Stacey Abrams. She did a good job. I congratulate her, but it was done in such a way that we can't let this stuff happen.

Donald Trump: (49:53)
We won't have a country of it happens. As a result Georgia's absentee ballot rejection rate was more than 10 times lower than previous levels, because the criteria was so off, 48 counties in Georgia with thousands and thousands of votes rejected zero ballots. There wasn't one

ballot. In other words, in a year in which more mail-in ballots were sent than ever before, and more people were voting by mail for the first time, the rejection rate was drastically lower than it had ever been before. The only way this can be explained is if tens of thousands of illegitimate votes were added to the tally, that's the only way you could explain it. By the way, you're talking about tens of thousands. If Georgia had merely rejected the same number of unlawful ballots, as in other years, there should have been approximately 45,000 ballots rejected, far more than what we needed to win, just over 11,000.

Donald Trump: (50:59)
They should find those votes. They should absolutely find that just over 11,000 votes, that's all we need. They defrauded us out of a win in Georgia, and we're not going to forget it. There's only one reason the Democrats could possibly want to eliminate signature matching, oppose voter ID and stop citizenship confirmation. Are you in citizenship? You're not allowed to ask that question. Because they want to steal the election. The radical left knows exactly what they're doing. They're ruthless and it's time that somebody did something about it. And Mike Pence, I hope you're going to stand up for the good of our constitution and for the good of our country. And if you're not, I'm going to be very disappointed in you. I will tell you right now. I'm not hearing good stories. In Fulton County, republican poll Watchers were rejected in some cases, physically from the room under the false pretense of a pipe burst.

Donald Trump: (52:03)
Water main burst, everybody leave. Which we now know was a total lie. Then election officials pull boxes, Democrats and suitcases of ballots out from under a table. You all saw it on television, totally fraudulent. And illegally scanned them for nearly two hours totally

EPILOGUE

unsupervised. Tens of thousands of votes, as that coincided with a mysterious vote dump of up to 100,000 votes for Joe Biden, almost none for Trump. Oh, that sounds fair. That was at 1:34 AM. The Georgia secretary of state and pathetic governor of Georgia ... although he says, I'm a great president. I sort of maybe have to change. He said the other day, "Yes, I disagree with president, but he's been a great president." Oh, good. Thanks. Thank you very much. Because of him and others. Brian Kemp, vote him the hell out of office, please.

Donald Trump: (53:05)
Well, his rates are so low, his approval rating now, I think it just reached a record low. They've rejected five separate appeals for an independent and comprehensive audit of signatures in Fulton County. Even without an audit, the number of fraudulent ballots that we've identified across the state is staggering. Over 10,300 ballots in Georgia were cast by individuals whose names and dates of birth match Georgia residents who died in 2020 and prior to the election. More than 2,500 ballots were cast by individuals whose names and dates of birth match incarcerated felons in Georgia prison. People who are not allowed to vote. More than 4,500 illegal ballots were cast by individuals who do not appear on the state's own voter rolls. Over 18,000 illegal ballots were cast by individuals who registered to vote using an address listed as vacant, according to the postal service. At least 88,000 ballots in Georgia were cast by people whose registrations were illegally backdated.

Donald Trump: (54:18)
Each one of these is far more than we need. 66,000 votes in Georgia were cast by individuals under the legal voting age. And at least 15,000 ballots were cast by individuals who moved out of the state prior to November 3rd election. They say they moved right back. They move right back. Oh, they moved out. They moved right back. Okay. They miss Georgia that much. I do. I love Georgia, but it's a corrupt system. Despite all of this, the margin in Georgia is only 11,779 votes. Each and every one of these issues is enough to give us a victory in Georgia, a big, beautiful victory. Make no mistake, this selection stolen from you, from me and from the country. And not a single swing state has conducted a comprehensive audit to remove the illegal ballots. This should absolutely occur in every single contestant state before the election is certified.

Donald Trump: (55:21)
In the State of Arizona, over 36,000 ballots were illegally cast by non-citizens. 2000 ballots were returned with no address. More than 22,000 ballots were returned before they were ever supposedly mailed out. They returned, but we haven't mailed them yet. 11,600 more ballots and votes were counted more than there were actual voters. You see that? So you have more votes again than you have voters.

Donald Trump: (55:51)
150,000 people registered in Maya Copa County after the registration deadline. 103,000 ballots in the county were sent for electronic adjudication with no Republican observers. In Clark County, Nevada, the accuracy settings on signature verification machines were purposely lowered before they were used to count over 130,000 ballots. If you signed your name as Santa Claus, it would go through. There were also more than 42,000 double votes in Nevada. Over 150,000 people were hurt so badly by what took place. And 1500 ballots were cast by individuals whose names and dates of birth match Nevada residents who died in 2020, prior to November 3rd election. More than 8,000 votes were cast by individuals who had no address and probably didn't live there. The margin in Nevada is down at a very low number. Any of these things would have taken

care of the situation. We would have won-

Donald Trump: (57:03)
Any of these things would have taken care of the situation. We would have won Nevada also. Every one of these we're going over, we win. In Michigan quickly, the secretary of state, a real great one, flooded the state with unsolicited mail-in ballot applications, sent to every person on the rolls, in direct violation of state law. More than 17,000 Michigan ballots were cast by individuals whose names and dates of birth matched people who were deceased. In Wayne County, that's a great one. That's Detroit. 174,000 ballots were counted without being tied to an actual registered voter. Nobody knows where they came from. Also in Wayne County, poll watches observed canvassers re-scanning batches of ballots over and over again, up to three or four or five times. In Detroit, turnout was 139% of registered voters. Think of that. So you had 139% of the people in Detroit voting. This is in Michigan, Detroit, Michigan.

Donald Trump: (58:08)
A career employee of the Detroit, City of Detroit, testified under penalty of perjury that she witnessed city workers coaching voters to vote straight Democrat, while accompanying them to watch who they voted for. When a Republican came in, they wouldn't talk to him. The same worker was instructed not to ask for any voter ID and not to attempt to validate any signatures if they were Democrats. She also told to illegally, and was told backdate ballots received after the deadline and reports that thousands and thousands of ballots were improperly backdated. That's Michigan. Four witnesses have testified under penalty of perjury that after officials in Detroit announced the last votes had been counted, tens of thousands of additional ballots arrived without required envelopes. Every single one was for a Democrat. I got no votes.

Donald Trump: (59:10)
At 6:31 AM, in the early morning hours after voting had ended, Michigan suddenly reported 147,000 votes. An astounding 94% went to Joe Biden, who campaigned brilliantly from his basement. Only a couple of percentage points went to Trump. Such gigantic and one-sided vote dumps were only observed in a few swing states and they were observed in the states where it was necessary. You know what's interesting, President Obama beat Biden in every state other than the swing states where Biden killed him. But the swing States were the ones that mattered. There were always just enough to push Joe Biden barely into the lead. We were ahead by a lot and within the number of hours we were losing by a little.

Donald Trump: (01:00:03)
In addition, there is the highly troubling matter of Dominion voting systems. In one Michigan County alone, 6,000 votes were switched from Trump to Biden and the same systems are used in the majority of states in our country. Senator William Ligon, a great gentleman, chairman of Georgia Senate Judiciary Subcommittee, Senator Ligon, highly respected on elections has written a letter describing his concerns with Dominion in Georgia.

Donald Trump: (01:00:40)
He wrote, and I quote, "The Dominion voting machines employed in Fulton County had an astronomical and astounding 93.67% error rate." It's only wrong 93% of the time. "In the scanning of ballots requiring a review panel to adjudicate or determine the voter's interest, in over 106,000 ballots out of a total of 113,000." Think of it, you go in and you vote and then they tell people who you're supposed to be voting for. They make up whatever they want. Nobody's ever even heard. They adjudicate your vote. They say, "Well, we

don't think Trump wants to vote for Trump. We think he wants to vote for Biden. Put it down for Biden." The national average for such an error rate is far less than 1% and yet you're at 93%. " The source of this astronomical error rate must be identified to determine if these machines were set up or destroyed to allow for a third party to disregard the actual ballot cast by the registered voter."

Donald Trump: (01:01:44)
The letter continues, "There is clear evidence that tens of thousands of votes were switched from President Trump to former Vice President Biden in several counties in Georgia. For example, in Bibb County, President Trump was reported to have 29, 391 votes at 9:11 PM Eastern time. While simultaneously Vice President Joe Biden was reported to have 17,213. Minutes later, just minutes, at the next update, these vote numbers switched with President Trump going way down to 17,000 and Biden going way up to 29,391." And that was very quick, a 12,000 vote switch, all in Mr. Biden's favor.

Donald Trump: (01:02:31)
So, I mean, I could go on and on about this fraud that took place in every state and all of these legislatures want this back. I don't want to do it to you because I love you and it's freezing out here, but I could just go on forever. I can tell you this...

Speaker 1: (01:02:52)
We love you. We love you. We love you. We love you. We love you. We love you. We love you. We love you.

Donald Trump: (01:03:03)
So when you hear, when you hear, "While there is no evidence to prove any wrongdoing," this is the most fraudulent thing anybody's... This is a criminal enterprise. This is a criminal enterprise and the press will say, and I'm sure they won't put any of that on there because that's no good, do you ever see, "While

there is no evidence to back President Trump's assertion," I could go on for another hour reading this stuff to you and telling you about it. There's never been anything like it. Think about it, Detroit had more votes than it had voters. Pennsylvania had 205,000 more votes than it had more, but you don't have to go any... Between that, I think that's almost better than dead people, if you think, right? More votes than they had voters, and many other States are also.

Donald Trump: (01:03:56)
It's a disgrace that the United States of America, tens of millions of people are allowed to go vote without so much as even showing identification. In no state is there any question or effort made to verify the identity, citizenship, residency, or eligibility of the votes cast. The Republicans have to get tougher. You're not going to have a Republican party if you don't get tougher. They want to play so straight, they want to play so, "Sir, yes, the United States, the constitution doesn't allow me to send them back to the States." Well, I say, "Yes, it does because the constitution says you have to protect our country and you have to protect our constitution and you can't vote on fraud," and fraud breaks up everything, doesn't it? When you catch somebody in a fraud, you're allowed to go by very different rules. So I hope Mike has the courage to do what he has to do. And I hope he doesn't listen to the RINOs and the stupid people that he's listening to. It is also widely understood that the voter rolls are crammed full of non-citizens, felons and people who have moved out of state and individuals who are otherwise ineligible to vote. Yet Democrats oppose every effort to clean up their voter rolls. They don't want to clean them up, they are loaded. And how many people here know other people that when the hundreds of thousands and then millions of ballots got sent out, got three, four, five, six, and I heard one who got seven ballots. And then they say, "You didn't quite make it,

sir." We won. We won in a landslide. This was a landslide.

Donald Trump: (01:05:43)
They said, "It's not American to challenge the election." This is the most corrupt election in the history, maybe of the world. You know, you could go third world countries, but I don't think they had hundreds of thousands of votes and they don't have voters for them. I mean, no matter where you go, nobody would think this. In fact, it's so egregious, it's so bad, that a lot of people don't even believe it. It's so crazy that people don't even believe it. It can't be true. So they don't believe it. This is not just a matter of domestic politics, this is a matter of national security. So today, in addition to challenging the certification of the election, I'm calling on Congress and the state legislatures to quickly pass sweeping election reforms, and you better do it before we have no country left. Today is not the end. It's just the beginning.

Donald Trump: (01:06:37)
With your help over the last four years, we built the greatest political movement in the history of our country and nobody even challenges that. I say that over and over, and I never get challenged by the fake news, and they challenge almost everything we say. But our fight against the big donors, big media, big tech and others is just getting started. This is the greatest in history. There's never been a movement like that. You look back there all the way to the Washington Monument. It's hard to believe. We must stop the steal and then we must ensure that such outrageous election fraud never happens again, can never be allowed to happen again, but we're going forward. We'll take care of going forward. We got to take care of going back. Don't let them talk, "Okay, well we promise," I've had a lot of people, "Sir, you're at 96% for four years." I said, "I'm not interested right now. I'm interested in right there."

Donald Trump: (01:07:33)
With your help we will finally pass powerful requirements for voter ID. You need an ID to cash your check. You need an ID to go to a bank, to buy alcohol, to drive a car. Every person should need to show an ID in order to cast your most important thing, a vote. We will also require proof of American citizenship in order to vote in American elections. We just had a good victory in court on that one, actually. We will ban ballot harvesting and prohibit the use of unsecured drop boxes to commit rampant fraud. These drop boxes are fraudulent. There for, they get... They disappear and then all of a sudden they show up. It's fraudulent. We will stop the practice of universal, unsolicited mail-in balloting. We will clean up the voter rolls that ensure that every single person who cast a vote is a citizen of our country, a resident of the state in which they vote and their vote is cast in a lawful and honest manner. We will restore the vital civic tradition of in-person voting on election day so that voters can be fully informed when they make their choice. We will finally hold big tech accountable and if these people had courage and guts, they would get rid of Section 230, something that no other company, no other person in America, in the world, has.

Donald Trump: (01:09:10)
All of these tech monopolies are going to abuse their power and interfere in our elections and it has to be stopped and the Republicans have to get a lot tougher and so should the Democrats. They should be regulated, investigated and brought to justice under the fullest extent of the law. They're totally breaking the law. Together we will drain the Washington swamp and we will clean up the corruption in our nation's capital. We have done a big job on it, but you think it's easy, it's a dirty business. It's a dirty business. You have a lot of bad people out there. Despite

everything we've been through, looking out all over this country and seeing fantastic crowds, although this I think is our all time record. I think you have 250,000 people. 250,000.

Donald Trump: (01:10:05)
Looking out at all the amazing patriots here today, I have never been more confident in our nation's future. Well, I have to say we have to be a little bit careful. That's a nice statement, but we have to be a little careful with that statement. If we allow this group of people to illegally take over our country, because it's illegal when the votes are illegal, when the way they got there is illegal, when the States that vote are given false and fraudulent information. We are the greatest country on earth and we are headed, and were headed, in the right direction. You know, the wall is built, we're doing record numbers at the wall. Now they want to take down the wall. Let's let everyone flow in. Let's let everybody flow in.

Donald Trump: (01:10:52)
We did a great job in the wall. Remember the wall? They said it could never be done. One of the largest infrastructure projects we've ever had in this country and it's had a tremendous impact and we got rid of catch and release, we got rid of all of the stuff that we had to live with. But now the caravans, they think Biden's getting in, the caravans are forming again. They want to come in again and rip off our country. Can't let it happen. As this enormous crowd shows, we have truth and justice on our side. We have a deep and enduring love for America in our hearts. We love our country. We have overwhelming pride in this great country, and we have it deep in our souls. Together we are determined to defend and preserve government of the people, by the people and for the people.

Donald Trump: (01:11:44)
Our brightest days are before us, our greatest achievements still wait. I think one of our great achievements will be election security because nobody until I came along, had any idea how corrupt our elections were. And again, most people would stand there at 9:00 in the evening and say, "I want to thank you very much," and they go off to some other life, but I said, "Something's wrong here. Something's really wrong. Can't have happened." And we fight. We fight like Hell and if you don't fight like Hell, you're not going to have a country anymore.

Donald Trump: (01:12:21)
Our exciting adventures and boldest endeavors have not yet begun. My fellow Americans for our movement, for our children and for our beloved country and I say this, despite all that's happened, the best is yet to come.

Donald Trump: (01:12:43)
So we're going to, we're going to walk down Pennsylvania Avenue, I love Pennsylvania Avenue, and we're going to the Capitol and we're going to try and give... The Democrats are hopeless. They're never voting for anything, not even one vote. But we're going to try and give our Republicans, the weak ones, because the strong ones don't need any of our help, we're going to try and give them the kind of pride and boldness that they need to take back our country.

Donald Trump: (01:13:19)
So let's walk down Pennsylvania Avenue. I want to thank you all. God bless you and God bless America. Thank you all for being here, this is incredible. Thank you very much. Thank you.

www.ingramcontent.com/pod-product-compliance
Lightning Source LLC
Chambersburg PA
CBHW030024290326

41934CB00005B/480